THE TOOLBOX

You have the tools you need to grow,
survive, help yourself, and help others.

BY MEL O. DIAZ

DISCLAIMER:

Please know the author writing this book does not hold a health professional license, nor is she encouraging you to follow these recipes, ideas, or suggestions as your primary focus on how/what you should do. The author of this book is just an individual following her own experiences, and she shares her take on life with the reader. This book is meant for entertainment only and with the hope it can make the reader's day a little easier. The readers are responsible for their actions. They are ideas you can use, change, or combine with yours. Think of it as your best friend sharing her thoughts with you.

DEDICATION

For my son, who inspires me to be a role model each day.
I celebrate and admire your kindness, and your strength.

For my husband who always pushes me to reach for the stars.
I celebrate your grit!

For my mother, who helped me discover the first tools in my toolbox.
I love you, mom!

For my brothers who are my truest of friends. I am yours.

And to those grown-ups who, by reading this book,
will rediscover their toolbox within.

CONTENTS

INTRODUCTION

I thought about writing this book, thinking of how I could help other people make their lives a little easier during any problematic time and where to find what they need to do such a thing…

So, I started to think about myself and the struggles I had to confront. My father abandoned us. Life was a struggle; we lost all our belongings and had only tea and bread for dinner. Sometimes, I had to be in a position where I needed to help raise my brothers, take care of the house, and go to school. I was not even in my teens yet, and the more I dove into my own experiences, the more I started to think about other people's experiences.

My life was not easy, nor did I think it was as difficult as others. My mother had no fun going through all she did, having to feed three kids and work.

Other people have worse experiences than I did: more difficult moments, challenging situations, fear, worry, sadness, and loneliness. Yet, they managed to move forward and continue living their lives to become good examples in our society.

I am in a much better position today after several years. I am in my forties, married, with a family I deeply love, and living in a beautiful place, and yet, there are still moments when I wish my life could be easier.

I don't regret anything that happened to me. I wouldn't change a thing. All those struggles, the tears, the fears, the worries, the frustrations, and the unknown helped me learn and appreciate what I have every day and gave me the strength to always look for the positive side of things (difficult at times, I must admit.)

All my experiences are the foundation of who I am today. And digging deeper, I discovered that we face challenges that either make us stronger or else. Ultimately, it is about how we choose these things to affect us.

Some people have it easy, but how do we know it is true? Most people try to build a facade to make things look pretty, and others create a wall so no one can see what is happening behind the "stage."

The truth is that everyone in this world experiences challenging moments and has circumstances that are difficult for one reason or another. People don't feel loved, can't seem to get it right, and forget themselves and others.

Yet some say that if you are a strong person with solid self-esteem, you could navigate life most likely on your terms. They also say that life will be easier if you have enough money.

I agree and disagree at the same time. If you have strong self-esteem and good values, I will say yes! High self-esteem with no values makes you selfish and careless. And if you have enough money to cover your basic needs and some of your wants, you may have it a little bit easier.... not a lot, because money can't buy deep, honest feelings... you either have them or you don't.

On the other side, self-esteem is something that requires work. You build it throughout the years, from the moment you are born. And suppose you didn't have parents, guardians, or caregivers who took that responsibility seriously and are most likely committed to your development. In that case, you will need to work on your self-esteem yourself.

At the same time, money doesn't bring you happiness, but it certainly can help create moments of joy, and there is nothing wrong with that. Some people and even our society contribute negatively to the belief that making a lot of money is wrong and that you should feel guilty about it. I believe that making money is a good thing. The more, the better! But I am careful about why I think that way and how I use the money.

I believe that the more money you make, the better you can help others. It opens doors, allows you to make connexions to grow personally and professionally, and you can help others to do the same. It helps you to do acts of kindness here and there. If you don't have anyone to share the money with, all the money in the world won't mean anything. By sharing, I don't say you need to find a partner, husband, or wife. It means you need to find a way to share it. Kindness is the best option.

And it starts with you!

My mother would say.. if you are not kind to yourself, how can you be kind to others? The problem is that it is easy to be kind to others if you choose to be, and not that easy to be kind to yourself. We started learning about kindness in Kindergarten and talked about it during the rest of our school years. I am still determining if we all have that education at home, but has anyone taught us how to be kind to ourselves?

I used to spend much of my time trying to figure out how to help my friends. Help them with homework, fix relationships, and even help them at their jobs… here I can hear my mother's words in my Mind again. She used to say there is no way you will improve anyone's life if you don't take care of yourself first.

I understand many of my mother's comments now that I have a child. She will have a comment here and there, and I must confess they bothered me sometimes, and I wanted to hear them other times. I value those comments much more today than yesterday. I wish I had shown her that I appreciated them back then, too.

I am thinking… do we have what we need to go through life? How do we learn to be kind to ourselves? Do we need someone who can help us understand certain situations? Do we need someone or something that can remind us that YES, we have everything we need, but we forget sometimes we have it?

As adults, we have friends, books, and professionals who can help us navigate the different experiences we have and will have, but what do we have as a child? Whom do we have?

So when I started to write this book, I thought of adults, my friends, family members, people I have adopted as family, and even people I don't know. But as I collected my ideas, I kept thinking about how everyone in the world could be in a better situation or feel better if that wisdom was taught to us from the moment we were born. And that is when we must start understanding that we have all the necessary tools.

If we help our kids today to discover the tools they already came to this world with and how to use them, don't you think they will grow up more assertive, confident, loving, and caring individuals who will succeed in life?

We all have to deal with our feelings first and take action based on how we feel at a particular moment. Kids do not know what all of that means, but if we could put it easily, playing and learning and helping them to be confident and trust themselves to be able to handle any situation they go through, I am pretty sure they will start living their life with the "right foot" as they say.

Life affects people in so many different ways. From an adult perspective, and after being influenced by our own experiences, parents, teachers, friends, and other people's stories, we could all agree that life is complicated.

But life through the eyes of a child is not complicated. His experiences are just fun, unique, and new. They have no idea how to feel about what is happening around them other than experiencing true, open feelings. And I wonder; how those feelings can help put together our toolbox for the future. With the help of parents, caretakers, and other adults in a nurturing environment, that child will become a kind and strong adult and develop a more comprehensive set of tools that will help him navigate the ups and downs of life by himself.

Years go by, and as we grow up, we forget we have been putting together that toolbox with everything we need to survive. With everything, we need to understand our feelings and help ourselves by using some of the tools we have been developing. And once in a while, we need someone who reminds us we have that toolbox, and we have the right tool for the right moment, and it is up to us to go and get it.

But more often than not, we fail to rediscover that toolbox within ourselves. Either we try to find answers outside or give power to outside individuals, things, or circumstances to control how we should feel and what we should do.

Well, enough with that nonsense. It is time to wake up! It is time to take control of your life and leave behind what stops you from becoming who you are: a strong, passionate, kind human being. It is time to regain your power and ignore what makes you feel weak and powerless. It is time to rediscover your TOOLBOX!

I called anything I could use to help in any situation a "tool." Although some people may call them human qualities: "A human quality is something a person has that makes them human." Others may use the term "personal qualities or character traits": characteristics that make you who you are, including knowledge and skills.

I like to call them tools because I use them to help me achieve a result. A tool, by definition, is a device used to carry out a particular function. The function of these tools, in particular, is to achieve growth.

So, in this book, I am re-introducing to you, we will find some personal or human qualities and sometimes words that represent an action that needs to occur at a particular moment.

Here are some of those tools we will reflect on and review to use today and forever: the curiosity tool, the gumption tool, the never-give-up tool, the bravery tool, the kind tool, the relax tool, the strength tool, the positive tool, the realization tool and so many more. I will go deeper into some of them later on.

I decided to talk about some of those tools in this book, which will give you the strength to start your new journey of rediscovering and rebuilding your toolbox.

Soul, Mind, and Body.

Have you ever felt lost? Empty or sad for no reason whatsoever? Feeling blue when everything around you should give you what you need to feel great?

How about feeling that nothing matters and everything is the same? The uncertainty of not knowing what is going on with you and how to fix it creates an anxiety level that is hard to control. It is as if the world becomes a slow-motion movie, and you still have to move a hundred miles per hour with a blurry horizon.

Have you ever felt that your Body didn't look how you wanted? Or that your Body doesn't want to do the job to reach that point?

Have you ever felt that those wrinkles are not a sign of wisdom and just a sign of stress? Or suddenly, you are losing hair or increasing past your ideal weight?

I can't tell you how many times I have felt this way...

And there you are, struggling along with everyone else with image and weight and clothes. You search for miracle Apps to exercise, magazines about diet, healthy stuff, videos about holistic, green, organic, vegan, and who knows how many are "calling" you... sending the message to your brain: buy me! I have the solution! They are calling you, or at least that is how it feels, so you answer the call, buy them, try whatever looks appealing to you at the time, and quit on all of them with the same speed as you purchased them.

Have you ever felt forgetful? Or unable to think clearly or not able to focus? Have you ever struggled with the most simple daily tasks, unable to finish a single one? And there you are, trying to understand where the day went. How did time pass so fast? Why have you not achieved anything you needed to do that day? What about the things you have been trying to do for the past week or months?

Did you ask yourself why? How did you get to this point? When did you lose control of your life?

And one day, you ask that person you see in the mirror, who am I?

Still, your Mind can't come up with an answer... why? Because it is busy. Busy with problems, busy with worries, busy with everyday life, house, family, kids, husbands, wives, friends, co-workers, neighbors, work, cleaning, organizing, and whatever is in a fashion that day.

Your Mind becomes a roller coaster of ideas that follow different paths. They are not in order. They are all mixed up; they are there, and they are not. And so you act like a zombie trying to follow the moment and not in charge. That is because, at that moment, it becomes much easier to follow and try to achieve whatever is in front of you. After all, you fall into a hole that will require so much effort to get out, and staying there is more comfortable because it is a place that you are used to being... at least a place that you have been for a while.

A busy Mind makes it difficult to calm down. Staying still is not an option. And between your active Mind and tired Body, everything around you is frustrating, creates anxiety, and pushes you down.

A hectic Mind and a tired Body are dangerous combinations. You can't feel calm if your Mind jumps upside-down all over the place. You can't relax with a tired Body. You can't stay still to allow yourself to breathe and let the energy flow. You can't evolve.

Evolution has many stages. I believe evolution is growth. It is renewed energy, finding yourself, learning, making mistakes, failing, picking yourself up and dusting yourself off, helping others, caring, being thankful, loving yourself, and loving others.

Evolution is feeding your Soul what it needs to help you start over again.

If your Soul is tinted, sad, mad, and full of negative feelings, it won't be easy to let the light, the positive vibes, come in. And when I say light, I am not referring to anything religious, although you may want to believe so. But my message here is to let everything go.... it is about allowing yourself to receive the positive energy the universe has offered. That "thing" acts as an eraser of bad feelings, cleaning the air and fulfilling that space with gratitude.

So, let's dive in together to find out what we can do to reset our Soul, Mind, and Body.

CHAPTER 1

OUR BODY

You may wonder why I am choosing to discuss our bodies first. Or you probably already figured it out... The thing is that our Body is our alarm clock. It is the one in charge of giving us "the wake-up call."

Sometimes, you may not realize and ignore your Body's little signals. Our Body constantly sends signs such as dark spots under our eyes, minor Body aches, a headache, back pain, losing some hair, and an overall "I'm just tired" feeling… Sometimes, the wake-up call comes a little stronger, and we experience pains coming out of nowhere. Sometimes, we cannot concentrate or forget things; other times, it comes suddenly and more robust as a medical emergency.

Most of the time, we blame a lousy night of sleep, too much work, etc.. (I take my hat off to all parents who wake up three, four, or five times during the night to check on their babies or feed them and then go to work and get the job done.)

We forget how wise our Body is. Most importantly, we fail to listen and pay attention to our Body even before it gives us the "wake-up" call. I wonder how many people listen to their bodies and consciously react healthily. Our Body will tell us something is wrong and whisper, "Hey, you need to pause for a minute.." Or it may scream, "Hey you! You need to stop!"

It is essential to understand that it is getting late by the time our Body reacts, and the need to do something for ourselves before becomes more explicit. We have to be mindful of that call. We need to pay attention.

Get up, stretch, and move.

If we believe our Body is in charge of giving us that wake-up call, why don't we take care of it so it is healthy and strong enough to defend itself from any negative energy coming from outside?

We rationally understand our Body is the only one we have, and there is no replacement, no returning or getting a new one, and no possibility of purchasing another just in case we need it. Why don't we understand that keeping a healthy Body is the right thing to do? Why don't we realize that a healthy and energetic Body will allow us to enjoy each day?

Many people struggle with their image, and most will blame the environment, their surroundings, and even other people. I always wonder if it is a lack of self-esteem or an excuse for not doing the work, or is it something between those two?

Think; let me ask what part of your Body you like the most and why. What part of your Body do you like the least and why?

Sometimes, I wonder if we should go back to school and re-learn why each part of our Body, organ, bone, and neuron exists; we would see why we need to protect and care for it. Without our bones, we would be fluffy walking jello, unable to hold a thing. Each part of our Body has a reason for its existence. From our brain to our nails, our internal organs to our skin! We need them! We want them! Could we exist without some of them? Yes, we could. But is it ideal in today's world and the way technology is going? NO. Knowledge will give you the power to care about your Body. Unless you have no choice, and yet still, those who use extra help will probably agree that we need every organ in our Body.

In the medical arena, we can see many factors discussed on this subject, and being no doctor, I will not go there. However, if you truly understand the value of your Body, you won't mess around with it.

Think of the many things you like to do, and you need your Body to help you achieve them, from walking, hearing, seeing, tasting, touching, feeling, and so on to help you do the things you need and love.

All those things we take for granted will be impossible without a healthy Body. And it has nothing to do with image and beauty. It has only to do with life itself.

Even people with physical disabilities, no matter what the situation is, need a healthy Body.

I want to clarify that it is not about the "perfect" Body as commercials try to sell… it is about the "healthy" Body we all need.

You like to play; you need your Body. You want to dance, run, or jump; you need your Body. You like to work; you need your Body. You like to feel hugs, smell the flowers, taste new flavors, read a good book, and touch your loved one; YOU NEED YOUR Body.

I can't stress this enough. So if you want to enjoy life, you better have a healthy Body.

It is all about health. Beauty comes after if you choose to focus on that.

So here is the First tool of the day. Encouragement. The "go do it" tool.

As soon as you wake up, get up and make your bed. This activity will give you a sense of purpose. There is a speech by Admiral William H. McRaven (U.S. Navy Retired), who wrote a book about it. It is a fantastic way to inspire people of all ages to start a day with an accomplishment. And it is so true! It is incredible how such a silly thing can give you the first boost of the day.

So get up and make your bed. Then, stretch and start moving.

Whatever your morning routine is, adding some movement, call it soft or strenuous exercise, helps to continue with that energy boost.

Seriously, take a minute. Stretch, breathe, and stretch again. There is something about stretching that makes our Body start feeling alive. Our blood runs through our veins, reaching every part of our Body. It gives the power to start moving.

Stretching is a powerful thing. You may like to exercise by doing yoga, pilates, spinning, running, and walking. You may not want to exercise at all. However, if you realize that stretching is something that every single sport in the world requires, you may realize that it has to be necessary.

How to stretch is up to you. For me, it is the "When" to stretch that matters. Not only is it essential to exercise, but it is also more important to start doing it in the morning.

Then feed your Body! I like to have a cup of tea or coffee. I like fruits or yogurt or toast with cream cheese; before I am ready to start my work day, you may want to do the same or not. Now, I began to add a glass of water before anything else, and it worked wonders!

I know people who skip breakfast, and fast seems to be the way to go these days. Cardiologists may say you need to fast for fourteen hours from when you have your dinner to when you have your breakfast. I agree with this last one. It helps you maintain your weight and lose weight if needed.

You should not skip breakfast, in my opinion. I ensure it is light after several hours of fasting. Whatever you make about breakfast, please ensure it is healthy.

How do we keep our bodies healthy? Move and choose to eat healthily. You can decide to exercise or not. Practice a sport or not. I would say, MOVE your Body. Walk when you can. Avoid the car when possible. Walk to the next bus stop instead of stopping at the first one. Walk upstairs, downstairs, find a coffee shop a little further, and if you feel courageous enough, walk to the supermarket and bring a few things with you, using them as weights. I would say that a bag of potatoes is not a good idea! Think first. Test it while shopping and make a decision. Killing yourself is not an option. And using a bag of potatoes, for that matter, may not be funny.

Nowadays, many people work remotely, at home, from a coffee place, at the beach, or else; if you are one of those individuals, sitting for too long will make you tired. So, if you are a workaholic like me, set the timer and get up every forty minutes. When doing chores, think of how you are bending to pick up stuff, bend your knees, and use it as your exercise of the day. Grab something from a cabinet and think about stretching as you do it. Collaborate with your Mind to help the Body move.

There is a study about overweight hotel maids that when they were told they exceeded the U.S. surgeon general's recommendation for daily exercise, they started to lose weight. Some agree that the type of labor requires them to move in particular ways, and others attribute this to the fact that their perception of their job changed after acknowledging it was also a way to exercise. It could be a combination of both.

The whole idea is that you move to give your Body something extra to do each day. And most importantly, keep pushing on those days when you feel tired and have minor muscle pain because you are not used to this new way of thinking and doing. Remember your tool: Go and do it!

The Three-day GOAL

There are many ways to help you go through this. Set a Three-day goal. Once you reach it, set another three-day goal. And do it again once you get the second goal. After five times you follow the three-day rule, you will start breaking up the old habit and crafting a new healthy routine tailored by you just for you.

Don't overdo it. Just because you are inspired doesn't mean you will run a marathon from one day to another. Remember, take small steps. Babies start running later than they can stand up on their two little feet. Athletes don't win a medal out of the blue.

And most likely, you, the majority of us, are not athletes. But if you think like one, you may be one in the end.

The truth is that you have to focus on your own Body. Do what makes your Body feel comfortable, and do it consistently. Go by threes. Every three days, add a new challenge. Repeat. It will feel like part of your life in a little while, and you will ask yourself why you didn't do it before.

It might be more challenging for those who like to find ways to procrastinate, find excuses, and lie to themselves. So, look for help within your surroundings. Find nature near you. How can nature help us? If you live in a big city. There is No backyard, balcony, or terrace, but you may live near a park. Find it!

We are all part of nature; we need to connect with nature at some point. Feel the fresh breeze, breathe pure air, and listen to birds. Looking up to the sky through the green leaves of the trees is one of my favorite things to do. It makes me feel connected with the universe. When you are in sync with your Body, you are helping your Mind. It makes me feel hopeful. And even if you don't like nature, meaning you are not a bug lover like me, I suggest you try. Be a risk-taker! Sit on a bench early morning in a nearby park, or take a nap under a tree; do it! Your Body and your Mind will thank you for it.

Here are some ideas:

OPTION A:

Step 1: Stretch for 5 minutes

Step 2: Take the stairs instead of an elevator

Step 3: Walk an extra stop to get to the bus.

REPEAT

OPTION B:

Step 1: Stretch for 5 minutes

Step 2: Park your car a block before getting to your workplace

Step 3: When you get home, park your car and walk around the block before entering your house

REPEAT

OPTION C:

Step 1: Make your bed

Step 2: Walk around the block right after lunch

Step 3: Walk your dog an extra 5 minutes

REPEAT

OPTION D:

Step 1: Get up every 40 minutes and stretch for 5

Step 2: Walk to the nearest park, run for a minute, and walk back

Step 3: Eat a healthy snack

REPEAT

OPTION E:

Step 1: Get up 10' earlier and walk your dog for five extra minutes

Step 2: Walk two additional blocks, then take a taxi to work

Step 3: Take a yoga, pilates, fitness, or sports class once a week

REPEAT

MAKE YOUR OWN:

MY THREE DAY GOAL	
STEP 1	
STEP 2	
STEP 3	
HOW DID I DO?	

Our Body at work

Can you believe that in today's age, some companies still think they have authority over your Body? They hire you not only based on your mental abilities but also by judging your Body type and if you "fit the mold."

There are indeed certain jobs that will require specific skills and a Body that can handle certain activities. A teacher of mine in human resources used to say: hire the person based on the job description and do not adapt the job to the person. In certain aspects, there is a lot of truth in it. It is not because you like the recruit sitting in front of you or because it is a family member or your boss; you have to hire that person to cover an empty spot in the company.

There is a reason why that role in the company exists. It needs to be covered by someone who can successfully achieve that position's goals.

However, nowadays, some companies realize that by being flexible, they can incorporate someone into the team that adds more value to the company. Consider even creating a new position. Or they may be open to modifying the job description if that modification will increase productivity.

On the opposite side of this, and unfortunately, some recruiters will only hire people based on what they see. Handsome, beautiful, striking, good-looking, and fit should not be in the vocabulary in the human resources department. And those words should not be in your Mind when you appear for a job either. Beautiful and handsome don't do statistics, manage software programs, or provide excellent customer service. They don't move fast, carry heavy equipment, or save a life. They don't answer the phone with manners, walk a patient to the fitting room, or teach a child mathematics.

The looks: Some companies require a uniform to fulfill a position. Nothing is wrong with that as long as they don›t try to impose particulars, such as high heels, no eyeglasses, super-narrow waist, etc. If they do, you may want to think twice if that is a place for you. Not because they are looking to achieve «the look» but because they are not considering the person, just the Body.. are we a thing?

You should not focus on your Body type when applying for a job. However, it would help if you concentrate on a healthy Body so you can do the job.

Our bodies and our relationships

Well, it's a touchy subject here. How many relationships (friends, family, partner) do you have that struggle with weight? Did you ask yourself if that is a factor when defining your friendships? I hope not. But if it is, it may be time to ask yourself why.

In the past, the perfect Body was voluptuous; that was considered beautiful, the "norm," some may say. Still today, a muscular Body is the norm. But there were and are environmental factors that determined this. What was available to eat then differs from what we eat today. The jobs available then are different from the jobs available today. There are parts of our Body that we don't even use today, but our ancestors did. Doctors use these parts during reconstructive or cosmetic surgeries. Even our food education is different today than many years ago.

Everything has evolved, including us, not only our bodies but also the concepts of beauty throughout time.

And there are also different cultures around the world. What we consider the perfect Body here may not be in another country, and none of those is wrong.

Anna Ginsburg directs a great video called "What is beauty," showcasing the evolution of beauty since the 28000bc-2018ac. It is fascinating how we all fall into the trap of what we should look at rather than how we should feel.

How about sex? Another touchy subject. Stereotypes, commercials, personal trainers, and muscles are everywhere. Will you determine your sex life based on what society considers "great sex if you have a so-and-so Body.." rather than what you like? What is the norm for you? That is the question you should be asking. What attracts you? What makes you feel alive? What Body type lights that flame makes you want to jump in bed with that person?

Studies on evolution concluded that the attraction between men and women was mainly for reproductive goals. Women looked for strong and healthy men to be able to provide for and protect. Men looked for a healthy and resourceful woman to reproduce healthy children.

In an article by <u>Daniel B. Yarosh</u>, "Perception and Deception: Human Beauty and the Brain," he shares how human characteristics affect our selection of partners. He very well describes how men and women behave in leu of beauty and attractiveness.

Over the years, beauty and attractiveness concepts have evolved regarding why one would select one Body type over the other.

How attractive are you? It is all a matter of perception. Don't you think? Does it depend on who is looking at you? Or, how is your perception of yourself? And even though some may say we have a significant influence from our ancestors, it all goes back to YOU.

What is attractive to you may not be to me. And that is OK. The key word here is, once again, HEALTHY.

Exercise and proper nourishment are the main components of a healthy Body. It doesn't only make you feel good; you sleep better. It also helps with your sex life.

It translates to high self-esteem, feeling attractive, and increased stamina. If you want to try new things, a healthy Body will allow you and your partner to do that. And, of course, continue to feed each other with creativity, moments of happiness, and ecstasy. With a healthy Body, you have the power to last, the ability to enjoy, the power to play, and the power to create. And with that, foreplay becomes part of the game and increases moments of happiness.

If you are not there yet, imagine how it would feel. Imagine that sense of empowerment and ownership of your happiness with your partner.

So remember, what matters the most is being healthy so you can do things and live longer to enjoy relationships at any level.

Ideas worth sharing..

1. Smoothie recipe I love: Super food!

    - 1/2 cup beet

    - 1/2 cup carrot

    -1 cup orange.

2. Buy a calendar. Use it to set three days goals. (Don't use it to add more stress meaning work and obligations) keep this one separate form any other.

3. Shea butter for your skin.

Our Body and our emotional well-being

Let me start by saying that our bodies and emotions are deeply connected. They both affect each other in one way or the other.

Both are linked and will affect our lives for the better or the worse.

People who struggle with health issues need emotional reassurance and support because their bodies will affect their mental health and relationships.

More and more studies on mental health and well-being show how our Body connects with our Mind and vice versa.

The Canadian Mental Health Association says, "Poor mental health is a risk factor for chronic physical conditions, and people with chronic physical conditions are at risk of developing poor mental health." The association also focuses on preventing these issues, such as increasing physical activity, access to nutritious food, and social inclusion and support.

Once again, we go back to the basics. A healthy Body will be the foundation for our well-being and growth as individuals, personally and professionally.

Oh, DEAR... do I ever get tired of saying the same thing... hmm... nope!

Scientists, Psychologists, Psychiatrists, Behavioralists, Gurus, Chancellors, Advisors, Life coaches, and more continue to discover and understand how we connect with ourselves. There are new methods, old ones, and better ones that they all try. And at the end, most of them agree that something profound keeps us going, feeling, living life, and understanding who we are. And that knowledge, those discoveries constantly remind us we are a unity Body-Mind-Soul.

The more connected with yourself you are, the more comfortable you will feel in front of your mirror.

Over the years, I have tried different techniques to keep my Body as healthy as possible. I can't say I was consistent because I wasn't. I had gone to gyms, paid memberships here and there, had personal trainers, did it alone, invited friends, and had support groups to feed each other the energy we needed to keep it going. I will not say I have done everything, but I am close. Instead of dealing with the challenge of being overweight, I struggled with the opposite. Over the years, going through those many alternatives, I never did it because I was trying to get as healthy as possible. I recognized that I did it because of what society determined the way a Body should look. I did it because my partner liked me a certain way. I did it because I wanted to look like the models on TV or in sports magazines. In the end, I did it because of the looks.

One day, I was sitting next to a man on an airplane. He looked to me like he was in his 40s. We started to chat, and he told me stories about his wife, friends, kids, grandkids, the adventures in his past, and the new experiences he had planned for his future. He was sharing his life, and it didn't make sense to me that he was in his 40s anymore. But that didn't match what I was seeing. A man with a fit Body, a happy and calm aura, and a smile could light up the whole room. So I had to ask! To my astonishment, he was in his 70's!! Can you believe it?

And again, I had to ask! How in the world was he keeping himself this way? I told him: Oh my!! I have to start eating what you are eating! He laughed.

This conversation became a before-and-after moment for me. And it happened to be that the next week, I came across a magazine that showed the "blue zones" from National Geographic and New York Times bestselling author - Dan Buettner. His article talks about five places where people live the longest.

I learned so much about the commonalities among the different groups of people. It is incredible to see how people from other parts of the world and various cultures do not have the same access to food, work, and other things. Yet, they all eat healthy, primarily on a plant-based menu and all of the exercise. Now, not what most of us think of as exercise, like going to the gym or running- but they walk to work and do manual activities. Even though some embrace technology, when they can, they do things themselves instead of pressing the bottom and getting something done. Last, they all do a type of meditation, praying, meditating, nature walks, and surrounding themselves with friends.

For most of us, changing our lifestyle is hard. Who are we kidding? And once we start the process, it is easy to fall into the cracks.

It takes self-control, commitment, avoiding procrastination, believing in yourself, awareness, and understanding and comprehending the pros and cons of your choices. If you need help, ASK! If you know of people trying to do it, join them! If people with a positive attitude surround you, stay with them.

On the contrary, if you spend your time with negative people or people who don't believe in you or your ability to adapt to the new you, RUN! Don't keep relationships that pull you down. If they don't share your way of living, it is OK. It is just not for you. It doesn't mean they don't love you. It just means they don't know better or don't want you to change because they may think they can lose you.

But it is not them who you should focus on; it is YOU. You are the one who will succeed. You are the one who, at the end or through the process, will inspire others to join you. If they don't like it, so be it! Either they want to be you, like what you have and do, or don't care.

The thing is that neither the negative nor the positive people are in charge of your life. You are. You are the one who has the choice. You are free to choose whether you take care of and protect yourself or not. And nobody can make that choice for you.

So, YES! It is super hard! However...

✦ One: it is not impossible.

✦ Two: It is worthy.

✦ Three: It is not only good for you but also your family and friends.

✦ Four: be the inspiration. If you can do it, others can, too!

✦ Five: you will be able to guide and help others

✦ Six: positive for you and the environment

✦ Seven: you are enough. Your emotional well-being depends on it.

With that said, I have a few questions for you:

✦ Knowing there is only one Body and no replacements, did you start the morning appreciating it?

✦ Did you wake up and say: I am grateful for today?

✦ Did you make your bed today?

✦ Did you move, stretch, or walk?

✦ Did you feed yourself a healthy breakfast?

✦ Just some thoughts…. If you get at least a "Yes" to one of these questions, you are on the right track already!

Congrats!!!! And Keep It Up!

CHAPTER 2

OUR MIND

Now that we understand the importance of having a healthy Body let us move on to our next challenge: Our Mind.

With a "real" active Mind, it is tough to pay attention to these events… because, well… your Mind is busy, HA! What is happening with your Body is bothering your Mind and vice-versa. Your Mind will block it and move on to the next thing. An overwhelmed Mind can give you a headache. Then, it will look for an easy fix. Any medicine you think will make you feel better… worthy? Definitely no! Falling into the trap of an easy fix will take you nowhere. You will be lying to yourself, giving power to an external thing to fix something that you need to heal from within you. What happens if you don't find an aspirin??? You will suffer for how long?

When our minds are busy with everything else, it doesn't have enough space to focus on our Body or listen to them.

Then the question is, why is our Mind so busy that it can't pay attention? Some people say it is because life itself takes you on a journey you can't control. Others will pretend it is work, family, or our surroundings, or they might say it is because you are using your Mind to cover the problem.

I tend to agree with the last one. I believe we are filling our minds with a lot of noise, so we don't have to take care of the real challenge.

Talking about the Mind is one of my favorite subjects. I believe we have "superpowers." Our Mind can control our Body, ease our pains, help us build our toolbox, choose the right tool from the toolbox, and develop moments of true happiness.

However, plenty of studies explain how our Mind works and that we are far from using it to its full potential. I ask myself if we will ever be able to do so. Nevertheless, we could improve and increase its capabilities.

I decided to call this book "The Toolbox" because I believe we all have a toolbox given to us at birth. Some tools come with us, and others we develop along the way. We use most of these tools as we are growing up. On any occasion, at any given time in your life, you will encounter a challenge, a fall, and a success. You can use a tool in your toolbox to help you embrace the moment and move forward. The problem is that we often forget we own this toolbox. We forget it is ready with the right tools, depending on the situation.

Here is where our Mind becomes the protagonist of the story. Our Mind is the one that needs to be focused so it can choose the right tool at any given moment.

We were born curious, brave, fearless, happy, and perfect. And as we grow up, we tend to listen more to others than ourselves. The knowledge and experiences we acquire throughout the years make us more cautious and alert, and we develop all kinds of fears that stop us from growing and evolving. I believe we can be who we want to be if we remember our tools and use them wisely.

In our everyday life, we experience different situations where something happens to us or witness something happening to others that affect our sense of self. We must share and remind those who, for some reason, are having a bad day about the tools that they also have to change their day for the better.

Sometimes, a co-worker may be insulted and hurt by another co-worker, the boss, or even a client. Sometimes, clients make us feel incapable because we are not fulfilling their expectations. Sometimes, our young kids wake up in the middle of the night afraid of the dark, a friend is going through a breakup, or a family member feels lonely. These are just a few examples of everyday experiences that affect most of us.

You and I could go on and on with many daily examples that require using the right tools to go through those moments, deal with them, and carry on.

I believe the most important and valuable moment is when we realize what is happening, acknowledge it, embrace it, and believe we can do something about it. This realization shows the right moment that choosing the right tool to work around the issue becomes imperative.

For these and many other reasons, we must focus on having a clear, quiet Mind.

You might be thinking: Ahh!, it sounds so easy, but how about you do it? It is not easy to put it into practice. And yes, you are right! It is easier to say it but never impossible to achieve it.

The problem is whether we forget we have the right tool for each moment or choose the wrong one. How do we know we chose the wrong one? Well, ask yourself: did I get out of my situation? Did I get the desired result, or did it make me feel ok? My answer will be to use your intuition. Deep inside, you know which tool is right and how to use it. Follow your gut, as they say. More on intuition later on...

So here is my Second tool of the day: The Realization tool.

It is not easy to reach the point where you finally realize you must do something. It requires deep thinking, self-evaluation, and the strong feeling you need to do something about it. We have to look for that feeling: the one that will get you up and make you do something about it.

I am not a Psychologist nor a specialist in any medical subject. Imagine a friend sharing what and how to use the toolbox when you read this book. This friend may have gone through similar experiences as you. My tools are the same as yours, and I sometimes forget I carry them wherever I go. But believe me, they are there. They are neatly organized and ready to be used when you need them.

When you recognize the moment and pay attention to how it makes you feel, your Mind will start processing the information and sending signals to your Body. Ask yourself these questions: Are you feeling tense? Are you in alert mode? Does this particular moment make you feel calm? Are you happy?

Here are two situations I would like to address. Those experiences will give you a positive or a "negative" feeling. I have the negative word in brackets because I don't believe in negative feelings. I instead call them "unpleasant" feelings. There are two things I want to emphasize about these feelings.

The happy feelings are easy to accept, but we tend to move on too quickly, and we don't give enough time for those feelings to settle so we can enjoy them for a longer time. If we do, this sensation will fill our Body, Mind, and Soul, making us more powerful against unpleasant feelings.

Yet, we tend to give more time, pay more attention to unpleasant feelings, and drag ourselves down the path of feeling even more miserable. Why is that?? Are we self-destructed human beings? Do we like the role of the victim? I get it, and I have done it. But realistically, it doesn't help you at all. It is a waste of time.

What is not a waste of time is to embrace that unpleasant feeling, let it be, cry it out, and let it go. Here is another secret about the realization tool. Suppose you realize you are embracing the unpleasant feeling. In that case, it loses its power and becomes a solid foundation for positive energy that will be useful next time you experience something similar. So be grateful you had it.

The thing here is that unpleasant feelings develop during a terrible experience, and sometimes they stay with us for a long time. As we move on with our lives, these feelings will reappear over and over while we live other experiences at different times as a vicious circle that is hard to escape. I am sure you know the sensations of those feelings, and you recognize them.

However, if you embrace them and accept or understand where they are coming from when they show up again, you will be more prepared to deal with them.

The secret is to do all that and let that feeling sink in; let it stay with you for a little while so you can realize why it is happening. Then you will know what to do about it. Once you accept it, be grateful for it. Understand that it just made you stronger. It magically added a new tool to your toolbox. And when similar situations arise, that unpleasant feeling will have no power over you. You will have control over it. Then, you can choose how you want to feel.

All feelings have different degrees of energy. The happy ones are the most important ones not to dismiss. I believe happiness is many "mini-happy" moments combined over time, and the more of these mini-happy moments you have, the happier and healthier Mind you will be.

Please focus on the happy feelings and be grateful for having them.

The most common fear is the feeling that something terrible will happen after the happy moment ends, so we tend to finish it ourselves "just in case" and start getting ready for the unpleasant feeling that is about to come!

Oh my..... As I write this, does it sound OK to you??? Are you for real?? Why in the world would you do that? Deep inside, I know, mainly if we dealt with bad situations before. We need to prepare for the next one so it doesn't catch us distracted, and we don't see it coming.

However, if we believe in ourselves, we will understand that if we go through something bad and are still standing, we will surely be able to handle it.

What do people say?..? what doesn't kill you makes you stronger? There has to be some truth to that statement. Yes, it is. You added another tool to your toolbox while experiencing something unpleasant so you can deal with another. So be strong and intelligent. Please focus on the happy feelings first and stay with them. Be grateful for them, so more will come. And during unpleasant moments, ask what you should learn from them.

Exercise one for our Mind: Breathe, Relax and Receive

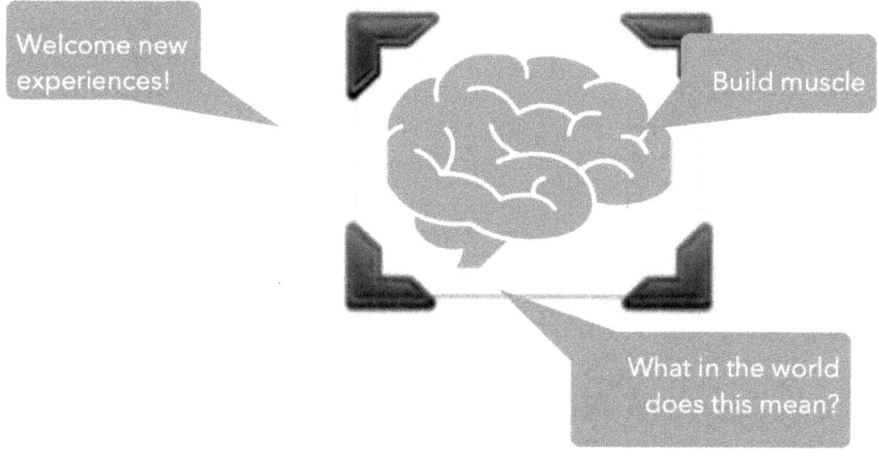

So far, we have taken action by helping our bodies get into shape and achieve a healthy state. Helping our Minds comes next.

Now, how can we help our minds to grow healthy too?

Think of it as if you were a hummingbird. Have you ever seen a hummingbird sucking nectar from a flower? North American hummingbirds average around 53 beats per second on routine flights. Our eyes can't even begin to follow them when they fly from one flower to another. However, once they choose one, have you seen how focused they are on feeding themselves? That nectar is not going into their mouth by itself. It requires precise movements and a sharp Mind to do it. Their wings are moving so fast that the human eye can't catch up with them. Yet they look as if they are floating still in the air.

That is how I like to think about our minds. But when our minds receive too much information, news, activities, responsibilities, and so on, how will we achieve this stage of moving and yet being still?

And by still, I don't mean suddenly becoming a statue so our Minds can relax. It will be funny to see a person instantaneously stop, not moving a muscle, because they need their Mind to relax.

We need to stop the noise at some point. Stop the nonsense. Now, this is one of the most challenging things to do. I love to work and love to be busy. However, being busy doesn't mean being productive. You can be active and achieve nothing at the end of the day.

So here is my Third Tool: The breathing tool.

I have always tried to learn how to meditate. I have tried yoga and nature walks and have never achieved more than a minute to calm my Mind. Until I learned about the importance of breathing, you may think there was nothing fancy about breathing. We all do. We don't need to think about it. On the contrary, taking time to breathe in a particular way is one of the most important things you can do to help your Mind relax.

Breathe. Just breathe. Breathe with a purpose. Breathe understanding and consciously do it in a way that will feel as if the world paused for a second. Feel the air entering your nose while expanding your lungs; hold for four seconds and exhale through your mouth.

You can do this technique, and you don't need any special training.

It is an activity you can do at any time, and nobody can't tell you this is prohibited.

We do it regardless. Why not do it with a purpose? Why not do it for ourselves? Why not do it as a reminder that we are alive and have to value each moment?

In the same way, we need our bodies; we need our minds. From the most insignificant activity to the most challenging, complicated, and demanding one, our minds are the engines.

Take a step back and think of everything you do during the day. Besides needing a Body to do it, could you have done it if your Mind didn't direct your Body?

Our Mind is a very complex thing. It took years for scientists, neurologists, psychologists, and other professionals to understand how it works, yet we still have a universe to discover. Many authors have written about the Mind of the human being. They are still talking and studying and will continue talking about it because it is so vast and complex that it will take years to discover its intricacy.

They all have something in common: they believe our Mind has not yet reached its full potential, whatever that might be.

One thing is true. Without a healthy, clear, alert Mind, we won't survive. So what can we do to help our Minds? Breathe to give your Mind a few mini-resting times throughout the day to recharge.

Let's focus on our Minds and what we can do about it. Start with breathing deeply one time, then another, and another... I like to follow the 4-4-8 technique. Breath in, counting til four, hold your breath for another four seconds, and exhale, counting till eight. After doing it a couple of times, you will start thinking about your breathing technique and the air that goes in and out, and you will forget for a while about those thoughts that keep you up at night. You will start to focus on yourself.

It is not easy for a busy Mind, I must say. At least it is never easy for me for the first couple of minutes, but I keep pushing through and don't give up. (Don't give up is a talent, by the way.)

And remember, you can do this anytime, anywhere.

It will help you relax. Doing it to assist your Mind to relax a little during the day will help you.

Following the breathing technique I mentioned just before falling asleep helps my brain relax and sleep better. I also like this idea because by letting yourself let go of all evil thoughts and uncomfortable moments you might have during your day, you clean your Mind to receive good energy.

I am referring to the positive energy the universe has for you. While doing this exercise, you will start feeling grateful. And gratitude is the most powerful feeling you can have. It centers you and makes you present. It helps you help yourself.

Allow yourself to receive that energy. That powerful emotional estate of feeling blessed.

Exercise two to help our minds: Make a list of ten things you are grateful for and stay with the feeling of being thankful.

Our Mind at Work

What can we say that you haven't heard before? Probably nothing… but it may be a good reminder that a healthy Mind will allow you to succeed at your job.

If you work in an environment under a lot of pressure and competitiveness among hard-core achiever piers. In today's business world, you must prepare everything for "yesterday." Today is already late. And if you work within the global environment, people are already waking up on the other side of the world when everyone is sleeping. So you push yourself to be ready, ahead of the game, because you want to be the first or because you have to be the first if you want to keep your job. (Sometimes not that well-paid job) …

It is true that if you work in the opposite environment, too relaxed, no push around, laissez-faire type of job, you won't push yourself more than what you need just because it is not required. That is not good either!

Extremes are never good. Balance is the key. And I can imagine what you are thinking right now; tell you what, in any scenario, you need a healthy Mind to achieve what you need and want, whether succeeding in the insane world of business or the laid-back alternative. More importantly, you must ensure you are not inside the hamster wheel. And for that, your Mind is the key to a happy work life.

In any case, the exercise of breading with a purpose (4-4-8) will be useful. Asking for clarity from the universe will allow you to believe in a higher you, and things and thoughts will come into place to move on with a clear path.

Our Minds and Our Relationships

At one point, love was one of the most searchable words on the internet. I wonder if it still is. Our minds get bombarded with the new realities concerning our health, the world's safety, and damaged communities, with people focusing only on themselves that they forget the neighbors or even friends who were "there" in the past but are discarded based on today's needs…

I can't believe how messed up the world of relationships is, but I am hopeful and genuinely believe that human beings are realizing more and more that we can't succeed in life by ourselves. We don't live on an island, and we are not alone. We need each other. We strive together. Think about it. Could you do all the things you do now without the help of others? Could you take care of a loved one if you don't have someone else's support to do the other chores you need to do?

Love comes in many different ways. So, let's discuss the connection between our minds and our relationships.

In an article by Scott Edwards, a science writer based in Massachusetts, he mentioned Richard Schwartz and Jaqueline Olds, Harvard Medical School (HMS) Professors, and their study on how the brain works concerning feelings of love. They study the brain of a group of individuals. When an individual sees pictures of someone special, the activity on the fMRI scans shows the brain more active in regions rich with dopamine.

Dopamine is a chemical related to the brain that makes you feel good. It allows you to feel satisfaction and motivation! It helps the nerve cells to send messages to each other. When you achieve something, you feel good! When you have sex, you feel good. You feel good when eating yummy food and spending time with a loved one.

And this is great! Of course, there is an extreme aspect of this matter. Some individuals fall into the trap of too much alcohol, drugs, and too many "love" relationships… Moderation and balance are key.

Did you know that dopamine also has a role in controlling memory, mood, sleep, learning, concentration, and Body movement? (There is a free service by the Australian Government where you can find more on dopamine.) They mentioned that dopamine levels could be adjusted, and since the brain is one of the main characters in this part of the book, we should learn more about it. Significantly because it can affect our mood, sleep, libido, and so on and if so, we all know that if we are in a bad mood, or don't get enough sleep, overeat, or stress, we won't have a good day with others.

This article I just mentioned tells you what we have been discussing all along… "healthy Body and a healthy Mind by eating habits that reinforce our health, exercising, and meditating."

Once you recognize that there might be a problem as to why your relationships are not working as you would like, think about what you can do about it.

If having great relationships makes us feel good, try to build, feed, and stay with them. On the other hand, if your relationships are causing you pain and stress, it may be time to switch.

How can we feed those relationships? Let's start with taking the step to work on what will make you feel good. Start with the easy ones; start with your friends.

🍦 Here are some ideas:

Family and friends

✦ Invite a friend to go for a walk.

✦ Send a lovely quote about friendship to a group of friends simultaneously.

✦ Share information that could be good for them.

✦ Use the actual phone and call. Strange right???

✦ Send a handwritten thank-you note after you are invited to their party or after receiving a gift.

✦ Hugs are magical!

Continue with your partner.

✦ Leave a loving note in a place where you know they will find it as soon as they wake up.

✦ Prepare lunch for work without expecting it

✦ Invite them for a nice meal

✦ Go for a walk

✦ Buy them a book,

✦ Find an item that will make them laugh

✦ Prepare a romantic evening

✦ Sudden hugs work the best!

✦ In the house, doing some chores will show you care

✦ Be funny, it works wonders

✦ Go above and beyond…

Following with your kids.

✦ Spend time with them without any electronics—no phones or computers. Just be there and engage in actual play and conversation.

✦ Ask questions that matter to them, not to you.

✦ Surprise them with a game in the middle of the day

✦ Take them to the park as often as you can

✦ Find out where they strive and help them to develop.

✦ Give them responsibilities and reward them.

✦ Create opportunities to play.

✦ Show them you love them; telling them is not enough.

✦ During hard times, the more love you show, the more they will trust you (I know; what are they pressing your wrong buttons? Oh well... what can I tell you? We have all been there, but remember, they are the kids and you are the adult)

✦ Read a book together.

The secret is doing it consistently, not just one time, to see what will happen. Use your Mind and find ways to repeat the action at different times of the day or month; do it more than they might expect.

Our Minds and our emotional well-being

Free your Mind and let go. Breathe, relax, and receive.

Will we ever get to understand and discover the human brain? Scientists and philosophers have been trying so hard to get answers to the most complicated yet simple questions that relate to our Minds and our well-being.

Remember, we are talking about the awareness of feeling "well" regardless of physical health.

This subject is complicated and non-talked-about, yet it affects many people worldwide and on many levels of our lives.

People feel alone, depressed, and anxious, unable to communicate what is happening inside them and express themselves; day by day, their self-esteem goes down, like in a twirled rabbit hole with no end.

People feel incapable of achieving anything from simple tasks to the most elaborate ones; they do not believe they are worthy of love, attention, friendships, or family.

The feelings of fear of disappointing a loved one, fear of the unknown, fear of themselves, and fear of being alone lead to depression and acts of self-destruction.

Mental health is a subject that was always been taboo. People call those who struggle with any type of mental health crazy! Alienating them from their circle of relationships, not knowing or understanding that, will make it worse.

As there are many levels of a mental health crisis, there are also many levels of comprehension. It is hard to explain. The suffering individual can't express what is wrong, and the individuals around them can't even tell if something is wrong sometimes.

The World Health Organization (WHO) reports, "Suicide is the fourth leading cause of death among 15-19 year-olds". It also says the link between suicide and mental disorders such as depression, alcohol use, the inability to deal with life stresses like financial problems, relationship breakups, etc.

Can it be prevented? In most cases, YES! And it starts by being able to talk about it. Even though the lack of awareness is accurate, some countries are working towards improving public mental health by eliminating the "taboo" impression and educating people about it. Companies are implementing well-being programs within their

Human Resources departments. As of today, thirty-eight countries report having a national prevention strategy, but there are over one hundred ninety countries, and we have a long way to go.

What is important here is the awareness, the wake-up call, the understanding and comprehension of the matter.

Suicide is one extreme of mental health, BUT NOT THE ONLY ONE. Many other levels affect everyone.

Don't be discouraged and avoid the conversation. Many feel lonely while surrounded by others. Engage in conversations and listen.

The US Department of Health and Human Services provides a little more color to what it is Mental Health: "Mental health includes our emotional, psychological, and social well-being. It affects how we think, feel, and act. It also helps determine how we handle stress, relate to others, and make choices. Mental health is important at every stage of life, from childhood and adolescence through adulthood."

And other than the typical suspects, such as family history and biological factors, life experiences are overlooked. If you visit their site and read the potential signs of a problem list, it seems that we all suffer from mental health issues at one point.

This article goes on to say you can cope with the stresses of life and work productively. Achieving and maintaining positive mental health will allow you to realize your full potential (many webinars about this subject, right?) and contribute to your family and community, which is true.

Your well-being is your most vital asset to succeed in life. It builds resilience and contributes to your full potential. There are so many things you can achieve:

- Overall enjoyment of life,

- Develop healthy habits, be more productive, connect with people better on a deeper level, lower your risk of illness, improve your immune system, keep you content, manage negative emotions better, and so on.

Keeping your Mind healthy and working on and towards your well-being will contribute to more and more moments of happiness.

Check	Here are some ideas:
	Stop and listen to yourself.
	Give yourself time
	Be patient and understanding with your mistakes.
	Failing is ok
	Learn from mistakes and be happy about them. Everyone makes them, but not everyone takes the opportunity to learn about them.
	Make your grateful list: I am thankful for my legs because they take me where I want to go. I am grateful for my senses because they allow me to see, hear, touch, feel, and taste all the beautiful things in life. I am grateful for what I have achieved so far. I am grateful for my failures; they taught me so much. I am grateful for the pains; they help me be resilient; I am grateful for the challenges encountered because they make me stronger and more forceful.
	Buy yourself flowers, a plant, or anything small that will add to your day to make it happier.
	Declutter your home.

Make your grateful list: I am thankful for my legs because they take me where I want to go. I am grateful for my senses because they allow me to see, hear, touch, and feel.

It is all about you! The world needs you. You are a piece of the universe puzzle. You belong. You are perfect. You are enough. You are loved.

Remember that!

Ideas worth sharing..

1. Breathing technique: inhale (four seconds) - hold (four seconds) - exhale (eight seconds)

2. Buy a small notebook to write the three most important things you need to achieve the next day. Not five, ten or a whole page of activities that need to be done.. You will work in blocks and achieve them. This is something I could write another book about block techniques to achieve your daily goals.. it is part of three ways you can accomplish your daily goals..

3. Hot chamomile tea before going to bed.

CHAPTER 3

OUR SOUL

B e grateful, Be present, Be you.

Think about our Soul as if it is a combination of little stars, tiny particles of energy that, as a whole, are connected and united, become who we are. Our Soul is like a blanket of positive, loving, and super powerful energy that requires us to feed it with more positive, constantly caring thoughts from a tranquil Mind with a strong, healthy Body to help grow and evolve.

If we could accomplish this, our lives would be perfect, and that is not the case. To feed our Souls each day and accept ourselves as perfect beings is complex. Let us say we are here today for this moment.

You are a perfect human being. True! However, the idea of perfection, an ideal Body, Mind, or a perfect Soul, is a work in progress. It takes time and everyday effort to keep up the excellent work. There is beauty in that! If we can visualize that "perfection" is what we want to achieve and set it as the horizon, we can always find ways to work toward that.

Realizing this fact, understanding it, and believing in it is the first step of what will take us on a journey where we become the drivers, not the passengers.

Remember: It is your choice.

By helping your Body and Mind, you start a healing process to help your Soul.

Have you ever felt confused, overwhelmed, and lost? And you start taking care of your Body and Mind, and still, even though you start feeling a little better, those feelings appear occasionally? Could this be another wake-up call? Another way the universe tries to communicate with us is to guide us in our evolution.

I always wonder if every single person has an idea of what their purpose is. Some people know what they meant to be from day one. Very early in life, others clearly understand who they are. The majority of humans don't have a clue. They think they know, but in reality, they don't. We believe we know who we are or want to be in society, norms, what we expect, and external influences.

When we are born, parents and family members think they know what to do with our lives and who we should become. And many of us follow. Not even questioning if that is really what we want to do and who we want to become. Fortunately and unfortunately, it takes a long time to understand the process, accept it, learn from it, and put it into practice. Some people don't even discover who they are, ever!

I hope that doesn't happen to you. I hope you either already know or are open to navigating the fantastic journey of discovering yourself.

Then the question is, what does our Soul do with all of this? Why is this important?

Does it matter if I was supposed to be a doctor, gardener, stay-at-home mom or dad, musician, or artist? And where is the line where a career defines us as who we are?

There is much confusion here. Who am I? You might ask yourself in front of that mirror. And those existential questions nobody can answer keep popping up in your Mind.

I tell you what; nothing makes sense if your Soul is confused or lost. Then, the question is, how can we help our Soul to be at ease, enjoying the journey of discovery..?

Most of our days, we run through those twenty-four hours without even noticing what is happening around us, submerged under pressure, obligations, responsibilities, deadlines, and appointments, and we fall into an abyss. Imagine ten years from today and look back. What if every day of your life was like that? How would you feel? What have you accomplished? How many moments of happiness have you collected?

There is another story from Psychotherapist Jorge Bucay. Did I mention that he is one of my favorite authors? He is. I met him in my twenties and then again in my forties. He and his son, both psychotherapists, have an arsenal of fascinating books with simple yet intricate short stories that anyone can apply in their lives. One of the stories is about how we live and treasure the happy moments in our lives. It is fascinating to me how much it applies to everyone. In his book: "Cuentos para Pensar," there is a story called "El Buscador." This short story is my translated version, but if you could, it is worth reading. So here we go,

"This is the story of a man we call a seeker. A seeker is not necessarily someone who always finds what they seek. A seeker is a person who is always searching for something.

In his path, he decides one day to go to the city of Kamir. So he packs his things and starts his journey.

On his way to the city, he finds himself standing in front of a beautiful park-like meadow. Beautiful trees, green grass, and a small bronze gate invited him to enter. Suddenly, he forgot about the city and decided to rest at that place,

Because of his nature, he decides to enter and, of course, investigate.

While appreciating the beautiful space, he couldn't help to notice white stones scattered around the park. He was enjoying the flowers, butterflies, and the garden itself when he saw an inscription on the white stone:

- Abdul Tareg, lived eight years, six months, two weeks, and three days.

A little overwhelmed, he realized that stone was not just a stone. It was a tombstone. He felt sorry, thinking that someone had buried a little boy there.

Looking around, he discovered that the next stone also had an inscription. He got closer to read it:

- Yamir Kalib, lived five years, eight months, and three weeks.

The seeker felt terribly shocked! That beautiful place was a cemetery, and each stone was a tombstone.

One by one, he started to read them. They all had a similar inscription: the person's name and time.

But what made him feel terror was that the person who had lived the most was only 11 years.

Overwhelmed by the pain, he sat and cried.

The cemetery caretaker was walking nearby and came closer. He looked at the seeker and let him cry for a while. Then he asked if he was sad about losing a family member.

✦ No, he said - what happened in this town? What is it with this place? Why are there so many dead kids buried in this place? What is the curse that made you build a cemetery for kids?!!

✦ The cemetery caretaker responded:

✦ You can calm down, sir. There is no curse. What happens is that in this town we have an old tradition... I will tell you.

✦ When a boy or a girl turns 15, parents give me a special gift, a notebook like the one I have on my chest. And it is our tradition to write down each time we deeply enjoy something. We then write on the left what we enjoyed and how long that joy lasted on the right.

The man gives examples like - meeting his girlfriend and falling in love. How long did that passion last? A week, two, three, and a half? - first pregnancy or the birth of your first child? How long does that joy last? - or being able to travel to that place you always wanted? Or the reunion with that sister who lived far away? How long did the joy last in every moment? Hours? Days?

Like that, we keep writing in our notebook, the caretaker explained. And he finished his explanation by saying the following:

When a person dies, it is our tradition to open that notebook and add the time of everything that person enjoyed so we can write on their tombstone because THAT is the only time we have lived.

.

..

...

I will leave you with a question: how long are you planning to leave? Better say, how much time are you REALLY living?

Our Soul, ourselves.

No matter where you are, with who you are, or what you are doing, you are you! And you MUST be true to yourself. You DO you!

Part of being true to yourself is to realize you are courageous. This realization is challenging whether you are a little kid or an adult. As a child, you need grown-ups to feed your self-esteem and help you realize you dare to do anything. It is up to the adult to know when and where to set up the limits as to where they let the child make decisions and try new things.

Oh my... If you are one of those parents who care so much about the well-being of your kids, it is a "humongous task."

Most kids have the willingness to try everything. As they grow up, they start hearing words like No, Be careful, You can't, It is too dangerous, That is only for adults, You are not a teenager nor a grown-up, Don't do it, It is too difficult for you, etc.

Those are tricky words! On the one hand, we, as parents, carry the weight of our parent's education, and at the same time, we must be protective. Just think how often you have been guilty of saying those words for a minute.

Do you remember if you said any of them and when?

.. Your child is at the top of the slide in the playground.

.. Your child is running toward the corner of the street

.. Your child is trying to cut meat with a knife at the dinner table

.. Your child is trying to solve a math problem that generally will be difficult for older kids,

.. Your child needs to learn how to go to sleep on their own

.. Your child wants to prepare breakfast and use the microwave

.. Your child wants to use your computer

.. Your child doesn't want to make friends, and so on.

It is a challenge that needs to be tackled and restructured to provide a more positive and cheerful environment for your children. Because courage is necessary for so many situations in life, starting young will help them develop a strong, healthy, kind self.

If we as parents can help our children understand the power of courage, how much easier will it be for them to navigate life?

The task is much more challenging for adults brainwashed by society or our parents and friends. See here; I didn't say "difficult" because that is not a word with a positive connotation. Even if you "know what I mean" as you read this. "Difficult" puts us already in a negative, defensive state of Mind. "Challenging," on the other hand, creates the possibility of a positive outcome. It triggers your sense of adventure to see if you can do it and look forward to achieving your goal.

So, if we try to be true to ourselves with little or no courage, it is the right moment to focus on that.

You see, nothing is impossible, and everything is worth trying. Within the law and safety parameters, of course.

It is crucial to surround yourself with all that positively feeds your Soul. To confront the fears and doubts and strengthen your Soul.

It is the time to auto-evaluate, self-check, and realize where we stand, where we want to go, and how we will achieve that.

You don't want to give your power to something or somebody to ruin your day.

Courage is a tool you can use whenever you need to.

Our Soul and Our Relationships

As I mentioned, we need to surround ourselves with people who encourage us to be better, constructive, and enthusiastic individuals to help us grow and feed our Souls with a positive attitude toward life.

Life is not easy, but it is worth living it! And when you fill your space with the people who love you and want the best for you, life is also fun, exciting, and thrilling.

By performing an auto evaluation, looking deep into ourselves, and understanding what our Soul needs to keep evolving, you will reach a point of realization. You will find the true meaning of love, friendship, and family.

Unfortunately, not all blood-related titles such as sister, brother, grandparents, cousins, or parents mean that they are suitable for your growth and evolution. Family comes first, but it is also true that they are not always family who will be there for you, nor will they encourage you to be better. Sometimes, you will be surprised and even disappointed that not all of them are happy for you when you achieve something. There will be envy, jealousy, mean intentions, lack of empathy, and many more bad feelings and surprising, not expected behaviors.

Here is when your courage comes to play the most crucial role. You will need that courage to stop those things from coming to you, even if it is painful and annoying to go through the uncomfortable moment to say Thank you, but NO, Thank you. With this, I don't mean you will have to cut ties with your family members who don't support your ideas and feelings. Well, maybe, yes. I don't know... you will be the judge of that.

To our surprise, long-term friends can also fall into this category. They share with you some of the best moments in your life or some of those fantastic events celebrating everything around you. They can turn into the ugly reality of disappointment.

We grow by building relationships. We grow with already-made relations, yet we must constantly remind ourselves that love is a giver, not a taker.

Start taking notes on who is there for you at any time: who shows up even if you haven't seen that person in a long time, who made that phone call when you least expected it, and who triggers your enthusiasm to live life to the fullest, who encourage you to achieve your dreams, which gives you a reality check and yet push you to keep going and try once more time. Start finding those family members or friends who constantly remind you that YOU can do it, that YOU should try one more time, and that YOU must enjoy the ride to reach the destination. Recognize the value in all of that and embrace it. Discard the comments from people who are only interested in your success if they see themselves touched by it, and forget those who look like they care but disappear when you don't give them what they want. It is "challenging" because it requires you to go through pain and loss and sometimes stay within the parameters of what we know; even if it is painful, it is more comfortable than the alternative. However, you must remember that lingering within the vicious circle is NOT your best alternative because it is NOT allowing you to be yourself, enabling your Soul to grow and learn.

When we think of trying something new, where the unknown reins, it triggers fears, nerves, and anxiety. Don't let those feelings stop you from trying because conquering them will allow you to be and experience a different life. A better kind of life.

You won't live in the past, and you will be able to start building a better and brighter future for yourself.

Remember, it is a challenge! And you will have to be strong enough to keep it consistent because living one way with the same people around us for so many years weighs a lot at the time to start changing.

But remember: change is good! And like my grandmother said: once you are on the dance floor, you dance! It doesn't matter how you dance; dance to the rhythm of your music.

Our Soul and our emotional well-being

We have skimmed the subject of wellness. We talk about feeling healthy physically and mentally. We touch the surface of how important it is to have a healthy Body, Mind, and Soul.

All those changes to get rid of people who are not a good influence, either because they encourage bad habits, stop us from doing what is best for us, lead us in the wrong direction, infect our lives with toxic thoughts and feelings, get rid of ALL of that will CHANGE YOUR LIFE!

And as an inevitable consequence, it will improve our well-being.

Every time we make even a minor positive change, our Soul smiles. Our surroundings become lighter, brighter, and with a sense of hope.

You will experience a glance at what the universe has to offer and how achievable it is. It is crucial to feel humble, forgiving ourselves, and letting the good, the light, Your God shower your day with love.

Your beliefs are only yours; I am not here to tell you who or what you must believe. But I can tell you this: whatever it is, it is there for you. It has always been and will always be: Call it God, Universe, or anything else. The bottom line is immense LOVE. It is your Soul connected.

We owe respect and kindness to each other, and we do so by showing up each day and being thankful for who we are, who we can be, and to all of those around us, past, present, and future relationships that help us be today the human being we are. We wake up each day being grateful for the person we will become thanks to everything we have learned, and we look forward to the future by living the TODAY.

CHAPTER 4

ONE TOOL AT THE TIME

We have introduced these concepts and learned more about our toolbox and how it will serve our bodies, minds, and souls. Hopefully, you have started to put some of them into practice already. If you did, I am sure you began to sense a shift in how you feel about your experiences throughout your day. You start to see things differently, acknowledge momentum, and change how you feel to have a more positive day.

How you feel based on the outcome of your experiences is based on how you approach them. Many times, if not most of the time, we are bombarded with situations we can't control, yet we feel the need to manage them. That is because we want to be in charge of how we feel, depending on the outcome. However, this is the wrong approach, I believe. Because no matter what we do, sometimes the unexpected happens, and we can't control the outcome. And if the result is not what we expected, we feel sad, frustrated, or angry.

Think about this, and ask yourself if you believe you could feel happier if you don't give power to a situation, a person, or even a thing to determine how you feel.

Those moments happen so many times during the day. You are driving peacefully toward your destination, and a mad driver starts honking HONK! Are they trying to get you to hurry up? Well, what an excellent opportunity to feel empathy! You don't know why the hurry or the madness. But instead of reacting with the same unstable feeling, which will lead to frustration and change the energy of your peaceful moment, just let the driver pass and wish him a great day.

How about when your day was not going how you wanted, and you come home, and your children start tantrums? Oh well, those moments at the end of the day. One of the hardest probably... It would be best not to succumb to reacting with the same energy. Sometimes, you must set the ground and find the way to do so; it feels impossible. Those moments are impossible to avoid. They will happen the same way other moments happen, and as hard as it seems, YOU CAN DO IT! Think ahead since you know your children and when these moments will happen. Modify how you approach these moments in advance. You could use happy and calm nights to teach your kids to breathe and control their temper, read books about it together, and when those crazy moments come, remind them of what you have learned together. It takes time for the kids to understand their feelings and why they feel that way.

Let's add a day at work where you didn't reach the deadline, your team didn't respond productively, or your boss is having a bad day and takes it on you, and, of course, a client complains about the service you provided. Great! Oh! And it has been happening for a couple of days. Now we are talking! Does it sound familiar?

Trust me, I know it is easier to say than do it. Even during those crazy-unstoppable-frustrating-pull-your-brain-out-need-vacation-days, it is still possible to find moments (mini-moments) to slowly but surely start redirecting yourself.

Going back to basics and being grateful is the ultimate way to go. Being grateful, you started your morning with two legs to stand up, have a bed and a house where you spent the night, and have food to eat and share with your family at breakfast. Be proud of yourself for being able to recognize you could feel empathy for that driver who was having a bad day. Being able to hear the birds singing on your way to work, look at that plant on your desk (if you don't have one, buy one! Great investment! It Not only cleans the air you breathe but also contributes to your happiness). Be grateful for having the honor to raise a child. And be thankful for your boss or clients complaining that if you don't take it personally, it will trigger the "Sherlock Holmes" in you trying to solve the mystery of the complaint and why it happened.

Let's review our ideas worth sharing and then discover what else we have in our toolbox and how and when to use each.

Body	Mind	Soul
Smoothie recipe: Super food! - 1/2 cup beet - 1/2 cup carrot 1 cup orange.	Breathing technique: inhale (four seconds) - hold (four seconds) - exhale (eight seconds)	Find something that reminds you to keep yourself grounded, well-balanced and sensible.
Buy a calendar. Use it to set three days goals. (Don't use it to add more stress meaning work and obligations) keep this one separate from any other.	Buy a notebook: write the three most important things you need to achieve the next day, Not five, ten, or a whole page of activities you want to do. You will work in blocks and achieve them.	Gratitude. Think of the three things you are thankful today for before going to bed.
Shea butter for your skin.	Hot chamomile tea before going to bed.	Trust the universe.

Ideas worth sharing..

1. Find something that reminds you to keep yourself grounded, well-balanced and sensible.

2. Gratitude. Think of the three things you are thankful today for before going to bed.

3. Trust the universe.

CHAPTER 5

THE GRATITUDE TOOL

READINESS TO SHOW APPRECIATION FOR AND TO RETURN KINDNESS.

Gratitude. This intense feeling fulfills your Soul because you have achieved, received, or you have the opportunity to give to others.

People talk a lot about gratitude. I always wonder if they understand its simplicity... because the truth is that it is not that complicated. Feeling grateful for whatever might be is easy. Unfortunately, the complex part is that we take things for granted; we forget to appreciate them.

The more complicated part is to be thankful during those moments when we struggle the most. When things don't go how we think they should, we get what we don't want to get and receive items later than expected, and people mistreat us when things don't go our way. As if our way was the right way... right?

How often do we want something so much and don't get it? Those moments are the hardest ones to understand, yet we can be and should be grateful.

You might be asking, grateful for what?? If I didn't get what I wanted? Why do I work so hard? For all the time I invested, and nothing happened? - let's be honest... when we are experiencing these moments, who is in the mood to feel grateful?

But the truth is that if you think about it, these moments are imperative to be grateful. And once those moments pass, it is even more essential to realize that they did happen for a reason. Maybe there was another door that opened; maybe there was another person you were supposed to meet; a better job came along, or you needed a wake-up call.

Could you have become a better person? Did you learn about patience? was that time to reflect and change directions? Only you know why it did or did not happen, and only you know how you will apply the knowledge you just acquired.

I remember once, I needed to park my car quickly to pick up my son at school. A man was sitting in his vehicle, wrongly parked. He didn't allow others to park behind or in front of him. I stopped my car next to his, lowered my window, and kindly asked if he could move his car just a little so I could park to pick up my son quickly. To my surprise, he yelled at me, sent me to where you can imagine, and gave me the finger! I was in shock! My Mind turned into a rollercoaster of thoughts. - I have to get my son. I needed to park somewhere and was about to be late... which is one of the last things a little kid needs for his/her caregivers at pick-up.

This man had the power to make that happen, but instead, he chose (after I explained why I needed him to move just a little) to make me suffer. In a fraction of a second, I needed to decide - either start a fight and try to make him move no matter what or let it go and keep going and find a better solution. And I was so close to responding to him like he treated me! But I chose to say, "Have a nice day, sir" (it was very hard, I must admit) and drove around the block. I remember being so upset for a few minutes until I asked what I needed to learn from this. Why did this happen to me today? I realized that tolerance was something I needed, and to my surprise, I found parking just in front of the door entrance of the school. And there I was, feeling grateful for my decision, thankful for the man who treated me with a total lack of respect.

Feeling grateful comes on many different levels, from the everyday activities or things we do to our most significant experiences.

Life is a challenge. And as such, being grateful could be a challenge, too, but it shouldn't. However, during extreme times, when we are dealing with our deepest struggles, unpleasant moments, and hurtful life experiences, we must try and find a way, a single moment, a spark in the day, something that makes us feel grateful.

Having been through dark moments, when someone said, "There are so many things to be grateful for," to be honest, the last thing we think is to find something to be thankful.. because our Mind, our Soul, and our Body are just searching to get out of that situation… the only thing in Mind is who in the world, I am going to stop this, how I get rid of these feelings, how can I escape from this situation, what in the world I have done to deserve this, I feel like an elephant walked over me. We continue feeding our Mind with all types of questions and comments that the only thing they do drowns us even more instead of helping us do just what we want to do: stop for a minute so we can restart, rethink, reevaluate… but being grateful is indeed the last if any, the thing we are thinking to be.

What if our parents told us at a very young age that gratitude is our tool, especially during those moments? Or trained from a young age to stop for a second and say thank you instead of complaining. What matters is that moment of stopping and feeling grateful because that is the moment at the beginning of turning things around. You don't have to believe me.

I invite you to try it. At any point in time, try it when your own parents are being difficult, when children don't listen, or when your partner is being selfish. Try it when you are having a bad day at work or when bad things continue to happen. Try it!

Be grateful for ANYTHING and EVERYTHING!

Let's think of some examples together: Breathing, having warm water to shower, having food to eat, a nice day, the person who waits for you at the elevator, the stop sign at the school corner, the restaurant owner who added an extra delicatessen for you to enjoy, the doorman who said good morning, the teacher who was there to explain and help you understand a subject, literally, ANYTHING!

I promise you better things will come.

Moreover, have you realized how many beautiful things you have and others may not? Start with all the things we take for granted. When was the last time you were grateful for those legs that help you move, hands that help you write, eyes that help you appreciate the colors of nature, and arms to hug and be hugged? How about being grateful to have a bed to sleep in, or a home where you can live, even clothes, so you are not cold during a cold winter?

When did you last feel grateful for the people around you who love you, your neighbors, your doorman, and even the delivery guy who ran under the rain to bring your groceries because you didn't want to get wet?

I encourage you to practice. It is great exercise! Keep thinking and be grateful for your kid's teachers helping you educate your kids, for the nurses and doctors you can call when you need them; be thankful for your teachers, your mentors. Think deeper and keep on going. Be grateful for the pets that keep you company, love you unconditionally, and for the places on earth you can enjoy.; parks, mountains, and beaches.

Be grateful for the no-so-friends who help you discover fake relationships versus real friendships. Those you thought would offer you an honest and caring friend disappeared when things got tricky. They help you today to cherish the real ones.

Be grateful for the hurdles, the pain, the loneliness, and the people who didn't believe in you.

All these triggered who you are today and show that humans can succeed and reach the final line. These are the moments in your life that teach you to push through. That when you push through, you become stronger.

Now, you don't need any other human being's validation. You need your own!

And when you show gratitude to the universe, you become stronger and more assertive and achieve small daily tasks. With each achievement, you prepare yourself for what is yet to come. You are prepared for your better self.

Now, you know it won't be easy. There will be times when you want to throw the towel and times when you want to kick a wall. There will be times when your sense of fear will start appearing, making you doubt the power of the universe. Believe me. I have been there so many times. If you succumb to those fears, you will only be delayed in what you should be. A delay you will regret if you don't challenge yourself and move forward.

It happens every day. The moment you start feeling confident, nothing will happen and that, will make you doubt again and again. Be alert that it doesn't become a pattern, and you will freeze in time. Remember, you can't control the clock. And if you want to achieve something, you take control of yourself. Allow yourself to take breaks is okay, but too long of a break or too many is not good.

You need to look in the mirror and say, I can do this. And imagine a better version of yourself and start working towards that.

I have traveled worldwide and seen amazing, beautiful things and painful scenarios. I felt happiness and sorrow. I struggled and felt powerless during a trip to Africa; I saw a child wearing shoes made from a car's rubber. I felt helpless in Central America and visited a school with walls that didn't reach the ceiling. Kids couldn't concentrate or learn appropriately because of the noises and people talking about different subjects simultaneously. To see mothers and fathers carrying heavy baskets of products to sell in the middle of a rainy day to have enough money to feed the families in the desert.

At the same time, I was amazed by the power of nature, rainbow-colored trunk trees, and miniature jungle frogs hidden in flowers. I was stunned by the elegant cheetah's walk, the beauty of an African sunset, and the power of the roar of a lion. I was delighted with the music played with flowers in the Caribbean, the beautiful smiles of little children who are happy just with what they have, and the kindness of elders sharing their food with strangers.

Traveling made me humble, and I wish everyone had the opportunity to do as much as possible. I hope you get to know different people worldwide, learn from their cultures, and realize we are all the same. Same bodies, same feelings, same humans. There is only one difference: those who are grateful for life are the happiest.

Gratitude is a powerful thing. It works in ways we can't even imagine. It helps us feel humble, sensitive to others, and blessed. It helps us keep those negative thoughts out of our system and liberate our Souls. Gratitude brings joy to your life.

Gratitude is all about being present. Not only physically or mentally. Be present in each moment in your life. Once again, it's easier to say than done! But we can always try our best and not give up during the process.

I discovered that by being present, the Soul, Mind, and Body come together, become one, and make you feel free. Free from people's thoughts about you. Free from limitations when it comes to your feelings. Free from strings of the past. And at that particular moment, You are You.

When you are present, you enjoy the moment. You live in the moment. And have the opportunity to appreciate everything and everyone around you.

It doesn't matter what people think of you or how they see you. It doesn't matter how society dictates you have to be. It doesn't matter. And you should not give anyone or anything the power to ruin your day!

The only thing that matters is how you see yourself and what you believe. You don't need anybody's permission to pick yourself up, believe in yourself, or feel grateful.

Special gift: Someone once gave me a gift. It was a word. It's one of the most powerful words I know so far. This a word and exercise that will make you stop being a follower and stop being affected by others (something you can't control). This will help you start focusing on yourself and be your leader.

Ready? The word is **OIL**.

You must be thinking about what oil has something to do with you. Follow me; imagine you apply OIL on your skin. Imagine a shower of oil. Any oil you want, any fragrance you like. Visualize the moment and feel it running through your skin. Every time you are in the middle of a situation affecting you in a negative way, and by that, I mean affecting your Soul, Mind, or Body in a way that makes you feel uncomfortable, here is what you will do. You will take a deep breath and think of the word OIL. And with that, all negative thoughts coming your way will slip away. You are in control. You decide how much those aggressive, uncaring, greedy, malicious people can get under your skin.

It doesn't mean you will stop caring about others; it just means you will not let others affect how you choose to feel, how you see yourself, and how you believe in yourself.

Here, we encounter a whole world of self-esteem. It is a subject of many books and seminars, a global issue, and we can go deep into a discussion. What I do know is that if you don't learn how to pick yourself up and continue your journey, you will never be able to succeed in protecting, caring, and loving your Soul, your Mind, and your Body. And as a consequence, you won't be able to care for others.

There are times when we need the help of others. Significantly when growing up. At other times, we need a little help from someone who can see us the way we cannot see ourselves. Sometimes, helps come from a friend, a coach, a teacher, or someone who cares about us. And sometimes, it comes in the shape of a book, a word, or even a movie. Help is always there if you put the question out there for the universe to respond.

However, the help we need comes from being able to discover the power within. Seeking and finding that power is a lifetime journey. Because when you think you have found it, new experiences and challenges come across, and you tend to forget you have that power within.

Remember your toolbox! It is filled with all the right tools to use whenever you need them.

Be grateful for the opportunity to feel grateful.

CHAPTER 6

THE KINDNESS TOOL

THE QUALITY OF BEING FRIENDLY, GENEROUS, AND CONSIDERATE.

As we start the day and practice and use the tools within our toolbox we mentioned in the past chapters, we will realize that those are not the only tools we have. There are many more and one for each occasion, depending on what we need when we need it, and why we need it.

Let's talk about a set of tools we can use for that extra daily boost that we can apply to any circumstance at any time.

Someone once told me: "Kindness is free. We just need to give it away," and why it is so difficult for some people to be kind to one another. Moreover, they are not even kind to themselves.

What can we do to explore the world of kindness?

There are so many daily examples where one can be kind. Say good morning to the doorman in our building or our neighbor. Let a person go first in the elevator. Open the car door so your partner feels that you care. Share your snack with a co-worker, and so on. It doesn't cost you anything, yet it fulfills the other person's day with a moment of happiness.

Be kind to your Body: treat your Body as a temple. Do what is right for your Body to keep it healthy so you can do things.

Be kind to your Mind. Try not to overwhelm it with things you can't control.

Be kind to your Soul. Give yourself time to meditate.

Be kind to the place we live. Ex. Plant a tree.

When can we do it?

There are plenty of opportunities to be kind. You have to choose to do it. You might be thinking, with all the things I have to do, I have no time to think about this, and I am not rude. Well, you are not being kind either, aren't you?

The truth is that the more opportunities you find and exercise the act of kindness, the happier you will be. It is not about the other person; it is about you. Being kind is being "cool." The kinder you are, the better your day will go, and slowly but surely, your day will change for the better.

There is a children's book called "Have You Filled a Bucket To-day? A Guide to Daily Happiness for Kids "by Carol McCloud. We, adults, should read it and often! We teach our kids what we should be doing ourselves. We should be the example to be followed. The younger generation needs us so they can also be examples for those who will come after them. If we want a kind word, we should start by being kind ourselves, period.

Now, have you been kind to yourself? When you wake up this morning and look at the mirror, besides being grateful for being under a roof and having warm clothes, you are thankful for being alive, etc. Have you told yourself you are proud of your achievements? How brave are you? How smart are you? Or anything that will make you feel happy about yourself?

So many days and months pass, and we don't hesitate to be critical and judge our actions, but we don't take a minute to be kind to ourselves.

Taking care of your Body, Mind, and Soul requires you to be kind and accept yourself. That will create a solid foundation to continue building upon and growing. It will become the core of your actions. And you will become someone who treats others the way you would like others to treat you.

You may not receive kindness from the same person you are giving it to; it doesn't matter. Being kind will make you feel good. And feeling good is the minimum expectation we should have the moment we step out of bed.

I dare you to try it! And observe. You will see how being kind changes your and other people's day.

Start with you. Then your family. Then, your neighbor, co-workers, the employee at the coffee shop, and even a stranger. Make an act of kindness your daily goal. And remember, you don't need to go above and beyond to do it. A simple smile will do it, too!

However, if you have already mastered it, challenge yourself to have a more purposed-like act of kindness. Show up unexpectedly to a nursery with flowers for its residents, bring school supplies on your next trip and bring them to the school that needs them the most, donate items or donate your time, and help pack items for emergencies.

Once you start doing this, you will find what suits you best and where you can excel in your act of kindness.

But most importantly, enjoy the journey! Because the results are always, always, ALWAYS positive!

Why should we do it?

It makes you feel good.

It makes the other person feel good.

It changes a negative moment into a positive experience.

It advocates for what is right.

It is considered a virtue.

It helps you connect with other people.

It boosts your confidence.

It contributes to a healthier and happier community.

Don't confuse kindness with weakness.

Being kind is not being weak. Being kind has nothing to do with pleasing or trying to be accepted by others. Those who are weak, harmful, or with low self-esteem often associate the two. It couldn't be the opposite! And I reiterate: being kind is being strong and positive and building your self-esteem.

The strongest the person, the kindest they are. There is the confusion that people often have. People associate strong with muscles and roughness and kind with weak, timid, or unsure.

It is a myth that you can't be kind if you are strong. It is a myth that you can't protect yourself or survive in this society if you are kind.

It is a fact that being kind requires courage, loving yourself, and caring about others. It is a fact that a human being can be kind and strong simultaneously.

You can set boundaries and gently say No. You can be direct, assertive, creative, challenging, strong, shy, outgoing, introverted, yet kind.

Remember, you can't be kind to others if you are not kind to yourself.

Practicing kindness is a gift. I hope you know it starts with you and then everyone else.

What is going to be your act of kindness today?

And remember:

It takes a STRONG PERSON TO BE KIND.

Things you may like to know:

- Song: "It's Cool To Be Kind" by Waves Rush In

- World Kindness Day: November 13

- Flower: Bluebells represent kindness

Kindness is good for you, and it is backed up by science.

CHAPTER 7

THE GRIT TOOL

COURAGE AND RESOLVE; STRENGTH OF CHARACTER.

There is a story of one of my favorite authors, Jorge Bucay, who wrote books and books about this subject. For me, the one story that stood out was the story of an elephant in his book "Recuentos para Demian." I won't tell you the whole story but will do my best to replicate the overall message.

..Once upon a time, a baby elephant was born in a circus and tied up to a chain at a very young age. As baby animals do, this baby elephant was not the exception and wanted to run and play. But he could only do it within the range of the chain length. He tried to escape and pulled that chain over and over. Because he was not that strong, he could not pull strong enough to break that chain. Over the years, the baby elephant became a young adult; once in a while, he wanted to escape and run free, still tied up to that chain and still not strong enough to break it.

One day, a little boy passed by and saw the sad face of the powerful elephant. He was old. The boy stopped and asked the elephant why he looked so unhappy. The elephant responded: I am sad because I want to walk around, run, explore, and can't. I have a chain attached to this chair; I can't break it. "

To the surprise of the little boy, who stood up observing, he could not understand the situation. He only saw an enormous, strong elephant tied up to a tiny chain. In this little boy's Mind, he imagines the elephant pulling his leg up and breaking the chain. So he asked: why you don't pull your leg up and go? The elephant responded: I can't. I tried several times over the years and couldn't do it. So I already know I won't be able to do it. I can't. So the little boy asked, why you don't try again?

At this point, you already get the idea. It is not that we can't; sometimes, it is about trying even when we think we can't, even when we have attempted to before. Success is just on the other side from the last time you tried. So try again.

The secret to me is telling yourself: DON'T GIVE UP! Pick yourself up and try all over again. The problem is that we get bruised, which hurts as we keep trying; it hurts badly sometimes.

Raise your hand if you ever have the feeling or even say aloud: "I'm done... really.. I AM DONE". It happens all the time, within our family, between other people, with ourselves at work, and within our professions.

Relationships are the most challenging situations because we are emotionally involved. Getting up and trying again after it didn't work after our feelings are hurt, is one of the most challenging things to do. However, would you rather say I won't experience love to the fullest because I don't want to try again? I don't think so.

Would you rather be alone than have friends? Would you rather keep your guard up and not be able to feel the full extent of being alive?

Then comes the professional bumps on the road. So many forks while developing our careers, and once we find a comfortable place, we stop trying for something better. Being uncomfortable is knowing you don't know everything, accepting it, and keeping on looking for something better.

If you are struggling with not being able to achieve your professional goals, tired that time goes by, and you are still stuck, give yourself a boost of confidence by not giving up!

Think about "What if.... " What is the elephant in the story pulled up that chain just one more time?

.. What if... you look at yourself in the mirror and say, "You can do it!" Come on! Try again.

.. What if... the next time you try is the right moment in time?

.. What if... the next time the right people surround you?

.. What if... the next time you are at the right place?

Or better yet, use the words: "Imagine if... "

Imagine if... the next time you try, your dreams come true.

Imagine if... this is the last time you have to try so you can move on to the next level.

Imagine... how you will feel after you try one more time and things start to move in the right direction.

Imagine if a better door opens because you just tried once more.

Imagine if you meet the love of your life the next time you try.

Imagine if... life starts being easy and you start feeling more confident. How many things could you accomplish?

Imagine if... you don't give up.

In the book "The Secret" by Rhonda Rymes, she uses the word imagine. I love that. Because when you imagine what makes you happy, it changes your attitude toward what you are experiencing. You can create your happy place, visualize, and feed yourself with happy thoughts—the perfect boost to your confidence.

Then, try to visualize and feel your thoughts if all those good things become real. A sense of urgency comes with this, the wanting to try again. We must embrace this feeling of success. And here, I am not referring to what most people consider success in terms of monetary reward. (I don't discard that either) But I am referring here to the results of the swift action from doing nothing else or giving up on the focus on our tool, "the grit tool." I am referring to the perseverance to improve, do, and be better. Don't be defeated by anyone or anything.

One of my favorite speeches is the one Angela Lee Duckworth gave during a TED TALK about "Grit: The power of passion and perseverance." She explains how she believes grit is a predictor of success. I love that she approaches this idea with kids and education, and after several years of research, she concludes that the grittier we are, the more we will succeed.

To add to her remarks, I believe we continue to experience failures and make mistakes. In those moments, you must take "The Grit Tool" from your toolbox, be courageous, and try again.

Do you remember having fears when you were born? We are brave by nature. We know no boundaries, take risks, learn, and try again. Sometimes, we need encouragement, and even though growing up, you may not get it from someone, you can find it by studying successful people and learning from their experiences. You will see they do have one thing in common. They know how and when to use "The Grit Tool." If you are reading this book, you know what I am talking about because you have experienced moments where you used this tool and sometimes forgot you had it.

As an adult or a young adult, you must encourage yourself not to give up. It would be best if you found ways to remember that failure doesn't define you. Failure helps you improve and prepares you for who you will be. Don't let those fears, bumps, and scars get in the way of your evolution.

If you are lucky enough to recognize this earlier in life, be kind and share the importance of never giving up on others.

If you have children around you, tell them the elephant story. Encourage them to keep on trying. When learning something new feels hard, find a way to make it fun and keep going. Once they achieve their goal, they will soon realize that the grit tool is one of the best.

Kids are very sensitive. Some more than others. Some kids put so much pressure on themselves that any failure could feel like the end of the world. Reminding them that failure or a mistake is needed to succeed is important. Those moments will make our little ones feel bad or feel embarrassed and upset. The way we help them get through those moments is what matters.

Understanding your child is not easy. The way we see and feel things today as adults is not the same way we feel or see things as children. Take a moment to yourself first so that with calm and understanding, you can guide and support your child. Bringing humor to any situation always helps. However, make sure the way you are handling them doesn't look like you are making fun of them. Kids are very self-aware and could cause the opposite reaction to the one you are looking for, which is to ease the situation and go over the main issue, which makes them feel one way or another.

Here is the opportunity for you to discuss subjects that matter. Nobody can tell you it will be easy. In fact, it will be a challenge for you and your child. For you, because you can fall under the spell of frustration and lack of patience. For your child, because he/she doesn't have the vocabulary yet to express what is going on or because those overwhelming feelings of distress and fear are taking over.

The good news is that everything becomes clearer and more manageable once this moment passes.

If we successfully come out of a challenging situation, we become stronger. Adding the "don't give up" and self-confidence and trying again or learning from our mistakes will enlighten our lives. We will become more driven, determined, and unstoppable.

CHAPTER 8

THE CONFIDENCE TOOL

HAVING OR SHOWING GREAT FAITH IN ONESELF OR ONE'S ABILITIES

Have you ever felt shaky, insecure, or self-doubting? Have you ever found yourself saying: I can't do it? I don't know why, but I can't do it.

Self-doubting is such a tricky feeling. It makes us hesitate and stops us from continuing to fulfill our dreams.

You should work on your confidence if you have any of these symptoms. Try to remember under what circumstances you feel this way. Do you see a pattern?

As painful as it may be, revisiting the moment that made you feel insecure and imagining a different outcome could work wonders.

You can do a couple of things to help you believe in yourself. One of the easiest ones is writing positive messages to yourself on paper, such as I can do it. I am brave. I am strong.

Each day, write a different one; as you write it, imagine the message entering your Body and running through your veins. Stick it on your bathroom mirror to see it first thing in the morning. Add that note to your desk or put it in your bag or pocket. As an amulet to protect against negative feelings, to stop that voice that says you are not worth it, you are not enough; after a little while, these messages will be within you, and you won't need a piece of paper anymore. You become your walking amulet!

Fill your Mind with images of successful moments. Visualize what you want to do and how you want to feel as if it is already a reality. Breathe deep and absorb the moment. Recognize that it can happen. Believe it will happen.

Visualizing and feeling happy will lead to taking the first step to rebuild your self-esteem. You don't need anyone to make you feel one way or another. You need you.

One of the problems I see while growing up is that we receive the implicit message that we need to make our parents and teachers proud. Sometimes, it is an innocent way to show that we care about your behavior and achievements. And believe me, don't get me wrong. Parents and teachers want to be proud of your accomplishments. On the one hand, it verifies that what they are teaching you is being absorbed and implemented. But how about we start teaching our kids to be proud of themselves first? And if succeeding in the children's goal results from a loving and caring life lesson or academic and sports challenge lesson, then... fantastic! However, confidence grows by realizing that regardless of the challenge, we try our best. And that is all that matters. It is finding a way to learn about our strengths and weaknesses. It is about making those strengths stronger and the weaknesses turning them into strengths.

It is about try and error. It is about figuring things out without rules to follow. It is about creativity and courage to try and not be afraid to make mistakes. It is about not being afraid.

Try saying to yourself: I dare you! I challenge you! See what happens! If you don't try, you don't know!

Most likely, and in most scenarios, the worst that can happen is that you could get a "no" for an answer, or someone will laugh at your comment (don't take it personally because it is not about you). That person who laughed probably didn't dare to ask the same question. If you remember the magic word: **OIL**, you can laugh together, and it will all be okay.

Trust me. Everything will be okay if you don't put yourself or anyone else in a dangerous situation.

See, one of my dreams was always to write a book. I started a few for the past twenty years and never finished them. I always told myself that it was a terrible idea, it would not be a good book, and what was I trying to achieve??… nobody would read it; I abandoned the dream.

Then, one day, probably five to seven years ago, I woke up from that dream again. I went back to my old notes. (I guess unconsciously, I never gave up the goal of writing a book).

This time was even worse. I was in another country, speaking another language, and my vocabulary had expanded, but yet again, I was not confident enough to start writing. I was unsure if my native language would get in the way because I wanted to write a book in English this time.

Some of you might be thinking, if you couldn't write a book twenty years ago in your native language, how could you write a book in another language? And that is what I thought precisely! So I started to doubt again, thinking I was not good enough, this is a mistake, you will embarrass yourself, so guess what? You got that right! I stopped.

Here we are, twenty years from the first time I thought I could write a book. I am writing a book and writing it in my second language.

What happens with all those insecurities, fears, and lack of confidence? I threw them out the window! I told myself it was enough!

I told myself: You can do it! Don't give up!

I remember thinking one day while training a group of employees and telling them we must lead by example. I was putting myself in the shoes of an "I never give up character" and trying to find solutions to what seemed to be a never-ending problem.

I went home, and something similar happened with my family; our motto is "We never give up." That night, I went to sleep and started to think if there was anything in my life. At that moment, I had given up… and it hit me: Writing a book!

And this time, I tap into my **toolbox.** I started digging for the right tools to help me overcome this fear and boost my confidence, and after using a combination of those tools, I began to write.

This time, the idea was clear. I wanted to write a book to help others, encourage them, and remind them that we all have the same toolbox. We can grab which tool we need at the right time.

This time, it was clear I would not give anything or anyone the power to determine how I felt about myself and others. Nothing has that power other than me.

This time, it was clear that I would start and finish writing the book regardless of what happened around us, other people's fears, or even my own.

So here I am, achieving my goal and trying my best.

Do I hope people will read it? Yes.

Do I hope it helps others? Yes.

Do I hope it is successful? Yes.

Then, I achieve my goal, and the results are fantastic!

Imagine if what you are reading now is not just a book but a best-selling one. I am imagining this myself right now! The thought of this put a smile on my face. It will mean that I have added value to you and other authors, professionals, parents, teachers, and all who work hard to bring something positive to this world.

Remembering you have a toolbox will help you move forward and start again. It will always help you.

Here is an idea:

I am sure you have a unique way of reminding yourself of things you need to do (switching a ring to another finger, tying a ribbon on your wrist, writing on a notepad, choosing an omen, changing things around).

Then, find something to remind you daily that you have a toolbox.

Go and pick up your confidence. Now repeat this aloud:

I believe in myself. I can do it. I am grateful for being able to do this (here, you will say what you are trying to accomplish).

This is my moment. This is me.

Confidence comes from struggling, going through a challenging time, and getting out of it successfully. So be grateful for the opportunity to show you can do it.

Now, go out there and start with your project again!

CHAPTER 9

THE BRAVE TOOL

HAVING OR SHOWING MENTAL OR MORAL STRENGTH TO FACE DANGER, FEAR, OR DIFFICULTY

How good everything till here sounds! But how good is it if we must be more brave to take action?

You see, in theory, everything sounds and looks great.

.. Of course, we need to take care of ourselves.

.. Of course, eating a healthy meal helps our Body and meditates our Soul.

Of course, imagining all bad energy slips away as if we have a coat of OIL.

Yes! Of course, the idea of being kind will make me happy.

Of course, achieving our goals because we didn't give up will build our self-esteem.

I don't know if you agree, but our previous experiences will form a foundation for our courage. However, how we embrace the results and those experiences feed our fears or trigger our bravery.

"If you fell from the horse, get up and ride that same horse again," farmers would say....

My grandma would say: "If you fall from the bike, get up and ride it again,"... and if you fall again, dust yourself off and try again!

Trying things that hurt us again doesn't mean you will repeat the same mistake. It will make you cautious, though, which is not bad as long as you don't become too cautious not to try harder. Learning from the experience is a great thing!

The issue is not letting those experiences stop you from what you can accomplish. They don't define who you are today, nor should they affect you negatively.

All your experiences are part of your life and help you become who you are. A person has many aspects; this is just one aspect and feature of a whole.

As you read this part of the book, I am sure that if you went through a very traumatic experience in life, you are thinking, yeah... sure.... Because you didn't go through what I went through.

And you are right. However, imagine that each human experiences things differently, and what is traumatic for some may or may not be traumatic for others. I am sure someone went through something more traumatic than you, and I am sure someone experienced something less traumatic.

So, let's say that we all have moments in life that we would erase if we could; yet again, remember that those moments help you be who you are and put you in a position to learn and teach simultaneously.

And the truth is that if you erase those moments, how could you have learned and helped others who got through the same experience?

See, regrets are not good. Don't hold on to regrets even if you lived a terrible life. Live your life to the fullest, happy or sad. Life is the accumulation of moments. Every moment is just a moment. When you look back at your life, even those sad times are just moments in the past. And if you focus on those happy moments, the feeling can last longer and replace the bad for the learned.

Being brave is the outcome of being scared about the unknown.

When we are kids, our monsters could be the dark, the noises, the not knowing what to do with our feelings, the nightmares, etc.; as we grow, and as teens, our monsters could be the feelings of not belonging, the fears of disappointing someone else other than ourselves, the pressure to be the best, the pressure of not being understood.

And then, as adults, those fears become our biggest obstacles. As adults, we carry those fears and add more: parenthood, pressure for being productive, earning a living, and being responsible for a family, and pressure for being a good role model.

It is important to understand those unknowns and learn more about what makes us scared and sometimes freezing without the possibility of not moving forward.

You can move forward once you confront your fears with information and comprehend why you feel this or that way. You will be brave.

Remember, someone always went through a similar experience as you. You can ask for help, and once you succeed, you can offer your support to others.

Because you are in a position where you were able to use the Brave Tool from your **toolbox**, you can now be in a place where you can help somebody else.

CHAPTER 10

THE STRONG TOOL

NOT EASILY INJURED OR DISTURBED

This is one of those tools that go together with believing in yourself. You must know and be convinced that you can do things you never thought possible. And the only way to test it is to try.

I am not talking here about being the queen or king of abs! Nor am I talking about being able to lift as much physical weight as you can.. The Strong tool is about being brave and trusting that you can handle the forces of the outside world.

This tool will give you opportunities to have experiences you never thought possible.

There are many ways the world around us can negatively affect us, and it is up to us to one: deal with it, two, go through the pain, and last, understand that you and you alone can handle it.

Many people have gone through different experiences where they thought, "This is the end," - "I can't do this anymore," - "This is too much for me," - and they end up being buried in their thoughts and feeling they are a victim of the circumstances.

Others stay still... they don't even try.... (Remember the story of the elephant?"

If you could get up from bed today, you are already strong. If you were able to wake up after a rough night, you are strong; if you were able to go through a scary moment, hospital, or deep sadness and are still alive, YOU ARE STRONG.

So give yourself a chance to test it, and you will see if you can do it. Whatever it is, you can do it. This tool is like fuel to a car. It keeps it moving. It helps that car to go from point A to point B. It will allow that car to go through bumps, curves, potholes, and even steep roads.

Same thing for us. The Strong Tool will allow you to navigate life like a pro. You will be able to find and utilize resources you will find on your way to your destination. It will help you go through dark moments and painful experiences in life for long periods, and even when you think you can't handle it anymore, this tool will keep you moving, and you will reach the end victorious.

Like all the tools we have been discussing, the thing here is that you need to remember you have your toolbox, and you have to use the tools you need at each moment in your life.

It is very easy to fall into the cracks and give up when things are difficult. Can you give yourself a break? Yes! But be aware that you can't take a break for too long because it will take more energy to come back up. If you don't let others get under your skin, you don't let situations you can't control upset you, you are helping yourself, and rising to the top becomes easier. This way, you can focus on your next goal.

When you allow anxiety and uncertainty to take over your life, the strong tool is the one you need to battle that.

CHAPTER 11

THE IMAGINATION TOOL.

THE FACULTY OR ACTION OF FORMING NEW IDEAS,
IMAGES, OR CONCEPTS OF EXTERNAL
OBJECTS NOT PRESENT TO THE SENSES.
THE ABILITY OF THE MIND TO BE
CREATIVE OR RESOURCEFUL.

There have been several studies on the concept of imagination. From the early stages of a human being to the versions of what an adult considers what it is to the point of belief.

Is imaging believing? Do we believe what we imagine, and when this imaging action goes from something fun to something scary to reality?

Apart from the medical aspect of someone with mental disabilities and what an ill Mind can imagine, which we will not discuss here, let's focus on the positive and what most people can apply to this concept.

Imagination is a powerful tool that can be used anytime during your day.

Because someone used their imagination, we have incredible books, movies, businesses, solutions, and useful items for our every-day lives.

Many inventors rely on their imagination to create and develop products to make our lives easier. Many scientists and professionals worldwide use their imagination to explore and experiment to bring solutions for humanity, save lives, fix problems, and protect nature.

Because he imagined it, Nikola Tesla created the X-ray photo. Because he saw his mother trying to find a better way to scramble eggs, he created what today is known as the "Tesla Turbine."

Because she asked questions and imagined solutions, Katherine Johnson helped to put the first man on the moon.

Because he imagined a warm home, Benjamin Franklin invented the Franklin Stove....

Because he imagined a better world, John Lennon wrote the "Imagine" song.

Because he imagined a better airline company, Sir Richard Branson developed Virgin Airlines and more.

Because YOU can imagine something, what will you create? What is in your future?

As they say... Imagine it, and your dreams will come true.

Imagination is the starting point to changing your life. It sets the horizon, the place in your future you want to get to, and you will work toward achieving that goal. Imagination allows you to think above and beyond your and anyone's expectations.

Without imagination, everything is almost impossible.

If you want to develop a new business, you will start by imagining what that business will do. Once you have your idea, you must plan to achieve your company's mission and where you want to go. Then, you will set up goals and plans and need to imagine how to accomplish them. How will you structure your new company to reach the horizon you already imagined?

To get in shape, you must imagine the Body you want to have soon. Your desired image, the shape of your core, energy, and how it will feel. How will you feel once you achieve the goal?

If you want to become wiser and generously share what you have learned, you have to imagine being able to help people. How will you impact those who need to hear you?

If you want to bake the most amazing cake for your child's birthday, imagine how it will look. You have to enter into the world of your child's imagination and combine your imagination to achieve her dream cake.

If you want to communicate in another language, you need to imagine traveling to the country you want to visit and being able to speak it. How many things will you be able to achieve once they are there in their native language?

You get the point. Nobody is born to be great at something, but everyone needs to start somewhere to be great. And if you can't imagine it; how will you start and stay focused on the path of greatness?

Only some believe this. That is OK. And often, it has to do with the fact that they imagine something which never came to fruition. Even after trying many times, jumping from one idea to another, one dream to another, nothing materialized.

Should you start the process again if you already know how it ends? I know... I have been there too.

Hear me out...

If you are not a believer, at least try it for fun!

First, it doesn't cost you anything. It is free.

Second, it is exciting to see the result you want to see materialize in your Mind.

Third, you have nothing to lose.

Fourth, it is only in your Mind and nobody needs to know… it is your secret to keep.

Fifth, success is around the corner; this is the corner you need to turn.

Last, remember the tool "never give up"? Yes? Ok then. Don't! Don't forget your dreams, and don't bring negativity to your life.

Instead, try again. You know what you want to see in your future. You know how you want to feel today and tomorrow.

So, when you are ready, follow these easy steps:

1. Find your place. Any place that allows your Mind to wonder: a park, a city, home, or even while walking.

2. Take a deep breath and exhale to eliminate the bad energy surrounding you.

3. Imagine something that makes you happy. It could be an activity, acquiring that gift you are "dreaming about," or giving your time to those in need.

Start to wonder how you will feel if you achieve your dream. How will the moment look? Who will be there? What will you be doing?

If you are still, close your eyes and visualize, step by step, what is happening at that time.

That's it! REALLY!

Secret: you need to do this every day possible. As much as possible. This exercise triggers things in our brain that will allow us to put things in motion. Our neurons will spark full of energy and positive vibes. You will feel the energy flowing through your veins, your chest will expand, and you will experience joy.

It is a blissful feeling you don't want to end. And you shouldn't.

Sometimes, guilt appears that makes us stop enjoying the moment, and a reality check shows up, and boom! No more happy moments!

Guess what? You can control that.

Guilt is a tricky feeling. In most cases, it has been imposed on us starting in our childhood. Sometimes, it is how parents control children and travel from generation to generation. (HEY! Wake up call here… if you have children, remember this. And stop using guilt to manipulate your kiddos). It backfires.

When guilt enters our system, it is difficult to challenge it, but it is not impossible. Hard, yes. Can you win? Absolutely!

If you have done nothing wrong, why feel guilty or underserved of happy moments?

Plus, who is "guilt" to enter your Mind when you use your imagination to feel better? OH NO, NO, NO! Guilt is not allowed in this process.

Tell yourself this is a safe space to create your reality. And make it one.

Once you enter into a good rhythm, you will find out it is a fun thing to do. And the outcome is only positive.

Once you experience achieving your goals and how that feels (even though they have not materialized yet), you will trigger the "Now I want to make it happen," once you get that idea in your Mind, you will start finding ways to make it happen.

And because it feels so great, you will put thoughts into action. Now, you have the train rolling to the best destination. The place you "Imagine" now starts changing colors, getting closer and more achievable.

Remember, if you are not a believer, you do it for fun!

CHAPTER 12

THE INTUITION TOOL

A NATURAL ABILITY OR POWER THAT MAKES IT POSSIBLE TO KNOW SOMETHING WITHOUT ANY PROOF OR EVIDENCE: A FEELING THAT GUIDES A PERSON TO ACT A CERTAIN WAY WITHOUT FULLY UNDERSTANDING WHY

Oh, dear! This tool is the queen of all means—the strawberry on the cake, the top of the top.

Trust your gut! Pay attention to those peculiar sensations in your stomach, listen to your inner voice, and believe.

Intuition is like having a superpower! It is like having a personal superhero on call 24/7. My favorite tool of all. Imagine being able to ask questions and receive an answer every time or having a bodyguard always there for you. Imagine how that feels.

If we are only open-minded to be able to listen, how much can we achieve, or what mistakes could we avoid?

Intuition is there.

Some scientists believe intuition operates on the right side of your brain; some think it is as accurate as any other feeling, and others completely disagree.

This concept is confusing yet as clear as a glass of water. You either feel it, or you don't. We all have it and feel it at some point in our lives. And if we learn to listen to our inner thoughts, our bodies, or that "something" that provides a "note" when we most need it, we will soon understand how intuition operates.

Whether you believe it or not, there will likely be some recollection of a moment when intuition served you well.

You may have made a last-minute decision on not taking that job, crossing that street, going to a particular place, or entering that alley.

Maybe you knew your kid was about to fall before they did, or what was the right decision for your employees, or you knew to refrain from joining a particular group of people. Maybe you suddenly thought of a friend or a family member, and minutes later, you heard from that person.

You knew what was about to happen before it did, there was something wrong about a situation or a person, or you saw something right even when others didn't... "you listen to your gut."

Now, how easy or hard is it to be able to pay attention to our intuition? Intuition has a louder voice in those moments of our lives when we are calm and connected. We can hear it. However, when we are overwhelmed and tired, it gets more challenging to do so. But make no mistake! It is there; when you are down, touching the bottom, feeling blue and scared, that inner voice will appear magically, and you will feel it. Remember, intuition is always there. It is your superpower.

If you ever made a decision based on "your gut feeling," a "hunch," a "je ne sais quoi", you surely know what I am talking about; you know intuition exists.

I always wondered what our gut has to do with all of this. But it seems, based on some studies, that it has a lot to do with this; it is like our gut has a separate brain, connecting emotionally with our Body, and is how we "feel" the butterflies.

Intuition is simple, powerful, and direct.
You were born with it. We all have it.

Whether you need to open an exit door and walk away from your current situation, open a new door to new experiences, or trust you are on the right path to continue growing, intuition will show you the way.

Now, why is it so difficult to listen to your intuition? Have you ever wondered why you had an isolated, strong, and very defined experience with your intuition and you never again felt that connection? Or why are you connected with your intuition so randomly or so sporadically?

Some call it a connection with God, the Universe, or many other names. Some call it faith. I don't know what to call it. All I know is that it is there. I also believe it is not faith. Faith and intuition are two distinct things, in my opinion. On one hand, there is faith, a true belief in something bigger than us that somehow is taking care of and guiding us. It is related to hope. On the other, there is intuition, that "thing" that appears when we need it the most, that "thing" that makes us trust our decisions and actions and guides us somehow.

I have also experienced the feeling of absence when looking for intuition. I got confused, and faith, hope, and intuition blurred. And I have felt lost, too. However, I always knew they were there, somewhere inside me. And I trusted everything would be alright.

The issue is that we all start getting busier and busier at one point in our lives and lose track of what is important. Money problems, bad relationships, boring jobs, and wrong friends add up to a point where we no longer can hear ourselves.

We waste time on social media television, wannabes what we see, and forget it is not real. We fall into the trap of becoming addicted to the life others have instead of investing in our very own.

You see, wasting time on all of that versus investing time using the media, the tools to improve, to learn, to grow, is what got us into not being able to hear our intuition.

Somehow, you need to disconnect first from everything harmful to you. Easier to say than done, you may think… true! But not impossible.

A good way to start is by connecting with nature.

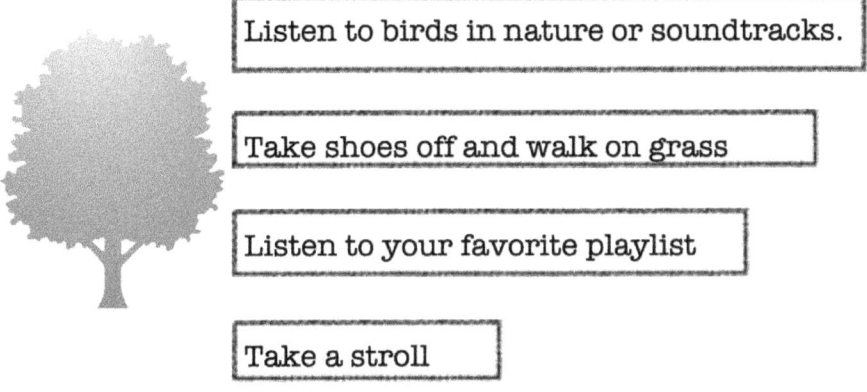

Listen to birds in nature or soundtracks.

Take shoes off and walk on grass

Listen to your favorite playlist

Take a stroll

Once you have done this, you can try exercise. Whatever makes you happy: yoga, pilates, boxing, you name it:

"Regular physical activity is one of the most important things you can do for your health. Being physically active can improve your brain health, help manage weight, reduce the risk of disease, strengthen bones and muscles, and improve your ability to do everyday activities." By the CDC - https://www.cdc.gov/physicalactivity/index.html

After that, do some meditation. Trust me, the sole fact that you switch gears, you start to want to hear your inner voice, the roller-coaster of thoughts in your Mind will start to slow down, and you can reconnect with your intuition.

While writing about intuition, I wanted to see if others share my beliefs. Individuals we know well who have succeeded in their field share their knowledge with the public and are not afraid to call it like it is. Individuals who also believe in Intuition.

I came across several people, some more famous than others, and overall, each has a similar view or feeling about this. I am sharing here some quotes about intuition:

* "..have the courage to follow your heart and intuition." **Steve Jobs** https://news.stanford.edu/2005/06/12/youve-got-find-love-jobs-says/

"Your conscience shouts, 'here's what you should do,' while your intuition whispers, 'here's what you could do.' Listen to that voice that tells you what you could do. Nothing will define your character more than that." "Follow Your Intuition." **Steven Spielberg** https://www.englishspeecheschannel.com/english-speeches/steven-spielberg-speech/

"I leave you with this: We are led by our gut instincts, our intuition, our desires and fears, our scars and our dreams. And you will screw it up sometimes. So will I. And when I do, you will most likely read about it on the internet. Anyway…hard things will happen to us. We will recover. We will learn from it. We will grow more resilient because of it." Taylor Swift https://www.elle.com/culture/celebrities/a40037720/taylor-swift-nyu-commencement-speech-transcript/

"There are times in all of our lives when a reliance on gut or intuition just seems more appropriate—when a particular course of action just feels right. And interestingly, I've discovered it's in facing life's most important decisions that intuition seems the most indispensable to getting it right." Tim Cook https://www.fastcompany.

com/1776338/tim-cook-apple-ceo-auburn-university-commence-ment-speech-2010

"With patients and in workshops, I listen with my intellect and my intuition, a potent inner wisdom that goes beyond the literal. I experience it as a flash of insight, a gut feeling, a hunch, a dream. By blending intuition with orthodox medical knowledge I can offer my patients the best of both worlds. Now, listening to intuition is sacred to me.." **Judith Orloff MD** https://drjudithorloff.com/do-you-have-intuition/

"If you have an idea that you genuinely think is good, don't let some idiot talk you out of it" **Stan Lee** https://www.facebook.com/benv.vietnam/videos/stan-lee-inspirational-speech/852605155234256/

"intuition is nothing more and nothing less than recognition." **Daniel Kahneman** https://fs.blog/daniel-kahneman-on-intu-ition/#:~:text=In%20Thinking%20Fast%20and%20Slow,note%20and%20file%20it%20away.

I could keep adding more quotes on Intuition.

The truth is that intuition is here to stay. More and more people are talking about it, from those highly educated to those without education, from professionals in different arenas to those in the trade business. Nowadays, knowing and learning what intuition is and what it can do for you is a skill we should cherish, learn, and respect.

As you can see, the bottom line is that intuition is believing and trusting your inner self.

It is in your toolbox.

CONCLUSION

You are you. A perfect human being with a perfect Soul, a perfect Mind, and a perfect Body.

This book is not meant to solve any problem you can not solve yourself. This book is meant to be one of those things you can have handy and count on each time you need that little push, that extra help, or that wake-up call. It is meant to be a place to rest, breathe, and relax for a little bit. It is meant to be a go-to book when you need some guidance, some kind of escape, some kind of "me-time."

It can be used as a reminder when you feel a little lost or desperate for an answer that you have the tools you need to make your life easier and to make you realize that you can do it.

I have a few books I rely on when looking for answers. I hope "The Toolbox" becomes that book for you.

As I am thinking about my last thoughts to share with you, these are the things that come to Mind:

- Take care of your Body because you need it, and it is your only one. So, Get Up, Stretch, and Move.

- Take care of your Mind because you need it. It is powerful and needs you to do extraordinary things in life. So, Breathe, Relax, and Receive

- Take care of your Soul because it is you. So, Be grateful, Be present, and Be you.

- Don't ever give up.

- Don't let anything or anyone define who you are. You are YOU. And you are enough.

- Believe in yourself. You don't need anyone's approval to love yourself.

- Be kind to yourself. Kindness starts at home. Once you learn to be kind to Your Body, Your Mind, and Your Soul, you will be able to be truly kind to others.

- Be proud of your achievements regardless of what anyone says.

- Don't give power to anything or anyone to determine how you feel.

- Be the example to be followed.

- Take small steps toward a big goal. Focus on the present.

- Any situation is an opportunity to be grateful.

- You have the tools you need to grow, survive, help yourself, and help others.

AND...

PST!

YES! YOU!

REMEMBER...

YOU OWN YOUR TOOLBOX.

REFERENCES

Page 15 - Admiral William H. McRaven (U.S. Navy Retired)

Page 74 - Jorge Bucay "Recuentos para Demian"

Page 77 - Rhonda Rymes "The Secret"

Page 77 - Angela Lee Duckworth gave during a TED TALK about "Grit: The power of passion and perseverance".

Page 23 - "What is Beauty" https://www.cnn.com/2018/03/07/health/Body-image-history-of-beauty-explainer-intl/index.html

Page 23 - Perception and Deception: Human Beauty and the Brain. https://www.ncbi.nlm.nih.gov/pmc/articles/PMC6523404 Daniel B. Yarosh

Page 38 - https://ontario.cmha.ca/documents/connection-between-mental-and-physical-health/

Page 26 - https://www.bluezones.com/about/history/#:~:text=He%20has%20discovered%20five%20places,%2C%20and%20Loma%20Linda%2C%20California

Page 41 - https://hms.harvard.edu/news-events/publications-archive/brain/love-brain

Page 41 - https://www.weforum.org/agenda/2014/09/understanding-human-brain/

Page 39 - https://www.healthdirect.gov.au/dopamine

Page 42 - https://www.who.int/news-room/fact-sheets/detail/suicide

Page 43 - https://www.mentalhealth.gov/basics/what-is-mental-health#:~:text=Mental%20health%20includes%20our%20emotional,childhood%20and%20adolescence%20through%20adulthood.

Page 47 - "Cuentos para Pensar" Jorge Bucay

Kindness:

https://www.mentalhealth.org.uk/explore-mental-health/kindness/kindness-matters-guide

Imagination:

Kid Scientists by David Stabler

https://www.fi.edu/

Intuition:

Intuitive Mind vs. rational Mind by Richard Branson

ABOUT THE AUTHOR.

Mel. O. Diaz is a woman, mother, and business individual focused on well-being and a positive take on life regardless of the circumstances. Growing up, she learned about the magic of believing in herself and discovering her toolbox.

Now, she finds the need to share her learnings with others, hoping to impact someone's life positively.

www.ingramcontent.com/pod-product-compliance
Lightning Source LLC
Chambersburg PA
CBHW051541120626
46551CB00013B/1326